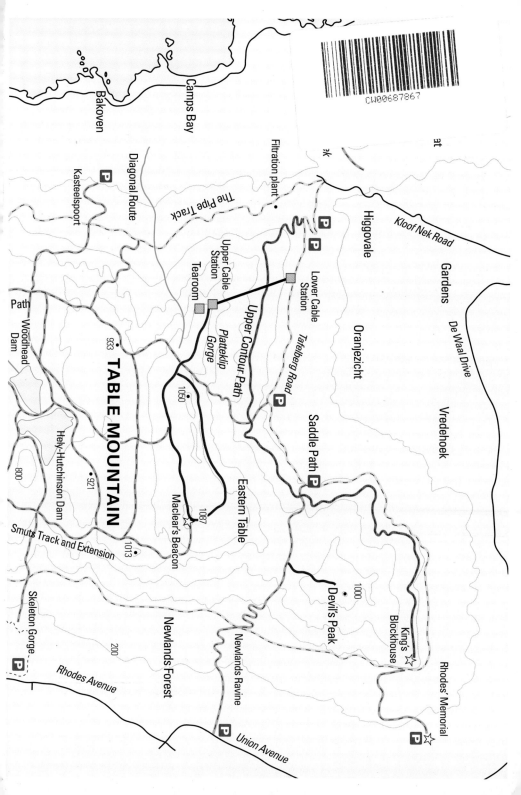

COMMON
WILD FLOWERS
of Table Mountain & Silvermine

Hugh Clarke, Bruce Mackenzie & Corinne Merry

Published by Struik Nature
  (an imprint of Penguin Random House (Pty) Ltd)
Reg. No. 1953/000441/07
The Estuaries No. 4, Oxbow Crescent, Century Avenue,
  Century City 7441
P O Box 1144, Cape Town, 8000 South Africa

Visit **www.penguinrandomhouse.co.za** and
  subscribe to our newsletter for monthly
  updates and news.

First published in 2007 as *Common Wild Flowers
  of Table Mountain*
Second expanded edition published in 2013

10 9 8 7 6 5 4 3 2

Publishing manager: Pippa Parker
Managing editor: Helen de Villiers
Editor: Joanna Ward (first edition),
  Joy Clack (second edition)
Design director: Janice Evans
Concept: Louise Topping
Designer: Beverley Dodd
Proofreader: Thea Grobbelaar
Indexer: Joy Clack

Reproduction by Hirt & Carter Cape (Pty) Ltd
Printed by Toppan Leefung Packaging and Printing
  (Dongguan) co., Ltd, China

(Print) 978 1 77584 039 8
(ePUB) 978 1 77584 082 4
(ePDF) 978 1 77584 081 7

PHOTOGRAPHIC CREDITS (in alphabetical order)
Shaen Adey/IOA (SA), Michael Archer (MA), Maré Ascott (MAs), Victor Barnard (VB), Matt Buys (MB), Hugh
Clarke (HC), Zane Godwin (ZG), Sam Greyvenstein (SG), the late WPU Jackson (with permission from his
daughter, Ms Rose Macmanus) (WPUJ), Rupert Koopman (RK), Sandy MacDonald (SMD), Bruce Mackenzie
(BM), Claire McCarthy (CMcC), Corinne Merry (CM), Sibyl Morris (SM), Gregory Nicolson (GN), Michael Nobel
(MN), Colin Paterson-Jones (CPJ), Sheila Robinson (SR), Bruce Stevens (BS), Chris Walker (CW), and Karen
Watkins (KW). *Photographs are labelled with the contributors' initials.*

FRONT COVER: Cape Scabious, *Scabiosa africana* (CM); (insets left to right) King Protea, *Protea cynaroides*
(CM); Painted Peacock, *Spiloxene capensis,* (HC); Red Watsonia, *Watsonia coccinea* (CM); Wild Aster, *Felicia
aethiopica* (HC)
BACK COVER (left to right): Silver Tree, *Leucadendron argenteum* (MN); Common Starheath, *Staavia radiata*
(HC); Cape Anemone, *Anemone tenuifolia* (CM)
PAGE FACING TITLE PAGE: Peninsula Silky Puff, *Diastella divaricata* (CM)
TITLE PAGE: Spider Lily, *Ferraria crispa* (CM)
THIS PAGE (left to right): Smooth-leaved Bush Bugloss, *Lobostemon glaucophyllus* (VB); Buttonhole
Saffronbush, *Gnidia oppositifolia* (CM); Red Disa, *Disa uniflora* (HC)
CONTENTS PAGE: Purple Watsonias, *Watsonia borbonica*, below the Twelve Apostles, Camps Bay (GN)

Contents

Acknowledgements

Our thanks to Yvonne Viljoen of the FOSNA Flora Documentation Programme who kindly gave us permission to use their map of the Silvermine Nature Area, which has been slightly modified for this book; Dr Bruce McKenzie, who vetted the botanical aspects of the original text, and to the many photographers (see page 4) who offered material. We welcome Corinne Merry both as author and as photographer of many of the flowers in this book. Her extensive knowledge of the flowers that occur in Silvermine has made this book possible. Thanks also go to Pippa Parker of Random House Struik and her capable staff – Helen, Colette, Janice, Beverley and Joy – who steered the book into production in record time.

Many other people contributed towards this book, not least our wives, Fenja and Doreen, who were supportive during the many hours we spent compiling this work, and Corinne would like to thank her husband Charles and her other hiking companions, particularly Ineke Moseley, for being so patient during the many stops they made while she was photographing flowers.

Any errors in the text or wrongful identifications are attributable entirely to the authors.

SM

The upper contour path leading from the King's Blockhouse to Platteklip Gorge

Preface

This book is aimed at readers who want to know more about the flowers they are likely to see along the many paths that crisscross the slopes of Table Mountain and Silvermine. The sheer diversity of plants is sometimes overwhelming. In the summer months the profusion of wild flowers is a joy to behold, made even better if you know what you are looking at. Any flower novice who hikes regularly will soon realise that some flowers are seen again and again. It is these common flowers that are shown in this book.

This book has as its roots a forerunner, *Common Wild Flowers of Table Mountain* (Struik 2007), a photographic field guide to flowers that are commonly seen. It was well received. Some readers suggested that we should put in even more flowers. This revised, updated and enlarged edition now contains 258 flowers, 60 more than the previous edition, as well as maps of both Table Mountain and Silvermine.

'Flower watchers' have a wide range of hiking trails to choose from and the most popular ones are briefly described in this book. The advantage of exploring the various footpaths is that the more areas you visit with differing habitats, the broader variety of flowers you will see. Every hike is a voyage of discovery. Please do not pick the flowers; take photographs only. The area is a World Heritage Site.

Our hope is that *Common Wild Flowers of Table Mountain & Silvermine* will encourage you to explore the mountains, enjoy the magnificent scenery and identify for yourself the many beautiful flowers to be found there. If this book helps you achieve this aim, it has served its purpose.

HUGH CLARKE, BRUCE MACKENZIE & CORINNE MERRY

HOW THE FLOWERS FOR THIS BOOK WERE CHOSEN

Table Mountain has some 1 500 plant species and Silvermine over 1 000 species. You may wonder: How does anyone know which flowers are most commonly found on the mountain? Bruce Mackenzie, one of the authors, spent seven years between 2006 and 2012 hiking all over Table Mountain making approximately 85 000 observations as to which species were flowering, where and when. When we compared his top 'most seen' 300 flowers with those of Silvermine, 87 per cent of those flowers were also seen in Silvermine. This is not surprising seeing that the two areas are adjacent. Corinne Merry, one of the key drivers of the FOSNA (Friends of Silvermine Nature Area) Flora Documentation Programme, has hiked in Silvermine for around 30 years and knows the area and its flowers exceptionally well. Based upon their data and knowledge, a selection was made as to which additional flowers to add to those already found in *Common Wild Flowers of Table Mountain*. To make the book even more interesting, we included a few 'specials' – beautiful flowers that are not all that common but are a huge delight when you discover them.

Table Mountain photographed from Lion's Head; Common Sorrel, *Oxalis pes-caprae,* in the foreground

Introduction

Table Mountain and Silvermine lie on Cape Town's doorstep. Nowhere else in the world does an area of such awesome beauty and rich biodiversity exist entirely within a city of 3.75 million people. Table Mountain is not only a World Heritage Site but, by global poll, was voted one of the world's new seven wonders of nature. It occupies an area of 57 km², with 650 km of hiking trails. Nearly one million people take the cable car each year to reach the top. The more adventurous hike to the summit or along the many hiking routes.

Adjacent to Table Mountain in the south is Silvermine, a protected conservation area. Although smaller in area than Table Mountain, its fynbos vegetation is rich in species. These include a surprisingly large number of endemics – species found nowhere else in the world – like the showy *Erica urna-viridis*, which only grows on the higher lying areas of Silvermine East around Muizenberg Peak, or *Erica nevillei* growing on Noordhoek Peak in Silvermine West. Other attractions include some indigenous forests, caves and spectacular sea views over False Bay in the east and over Chapman's Peak Drive and Hout Bay in the west.

For flower-lovers, a walk in these wild areas is an amazing experience year round, but especially during the spring and summer months (September to March).

We have included flowers that are generally attractive, eye-catching and easily seen. Flowers that are really tiny and less interesting, which the average hiker or rambler would usually walk past without a second glance, are not featured. A few really beautiful species, although not widely dispersed, are included.

The text is written for absolute beginners and has been designed to make flower recognition and identification as easy as possible. Where they are known, English and Afrikaans common names for flowers have been given, and scientific names are provided too. The flower descriptions have been kept simple – we avoided complex terms that mean little to those who have not studied botany. Words that appear in **bold** in the text are explained in either the text glossary (page 112) or illustrated glossary (page 113). A special effort has been made to catch the essence of the flower being described, and to record features that beginners would most likely note and that will help identify each flower.

Painted Lady, *Gladiolus carneus*   Autumn Painted Lady, *Gladiolus monticola*

Using this book

Photographs

Most readers will probably rely largely on the photographs provided to identify flowers; many plants are distinctive and you should have no problem identifying them in this way. The photographs are mostly close-ups, showing what you would see if you were right next to the flower, and some have inserts that provide a more distant view of the flowering plant.

The flowers are grouped together in sections according to their colour, and each page has a colour bar reflecting the tint of the flowers on that page; this makes it easy to find a colour match for any specimen.

We have grouped flowers according to the *predominant colour of their petals* (red, yellow, blue, etc.). Some flowers have a variety of colour forms; we show and describe the colour variant we found *most often* on Table Mountain and Silvermine, and also indicate other colour possibilities. If a flower has blue petals and a yellow centre, ignore the colour of the flower's centre and turn to the blue-coded pages. Remember that flowers' colours can vary and you may find specimens of a lighter, darker or even a different shade altogether from the one shown in this book.

Beneath each photograph is a tinted panel showing two further tools to aid identification of the species:

Flowering season

This reflects the months in which we, the authors, saw that species in bloom. Note that flowers may well grow outside these months, but if you have two 'lookalikes' and one is not meant to be in flower at the time you are looking at it, this may help identify the species.

Height

The height of each plant is given, in metres or centimetres. Bear in mind, however, that the height of plants can vary according to maturity of the plant, locality, frequency of fires, climatic variation and so on. We have used the term 'up to . . .' to accommodate such variations. In general, we have followed the heights specified in Goldblatt & Manning's *Cape Plants: A conspectus of the Cape Flora of South Africa*, moderated by our own observations of those plants we have seen on Table Mountain and Silvermine.

Flower descriptions

If you cannot identify the flower by looking at the photograph, read the text description alongside any likely photographs, which will provide the following key identifying features:

Leaves

Leaves are described in terms of *size* (large, small), *shape* (oval, round, sword-shaped), *texture* (rough, smooth) and *where they are* on the plant (high, low). Remember that leaf size is relative to the flower size – a 'large' leaf on a small-flowered plant may be described as a 'small' leaf on a large-flowered plant. Illustrations of leaf shapes are provided in the illustrated glossary (page 113).

Stonecrop, *Crassula pellucida*

Flower head

We describe the main features without going into botanical detail, using the term 'flower head' in its most general sense: it can mean a dense cluster of tiny flowers, but our description refers to the overall impression of the head, not the tiny, individual blossoms.

Distribution

Not all flowers are widely spread; some have very localised habitats. To indicate your likelihood of coming across the flowers in this book during the flowering season, we use the following terminology in the text:

Rare: Found in only a few locations.*

Occasional/Uncommon: Seen once in a while or somewhat irregularly.

Fairly common: Seen regularly but not in abundance.

Common: Often observed and widely spread.

Frequently found: This term is used when a species is very common, widely spread and abundant.

Red Crassula, *Crassula coccinea*

* Do not be disheartened if some wild flowers are indicated as 'Rare'. Although found only in a few locations, some of them, like the Red Disa, *Disa uniflora*, appear in the aquaduct area on Table Mountain in their hundreds. In other localities, like Skeleton Gorge and Myburgh's Waterfall Ravine, this is not the case.

Common and scientific names, and name changes

While common names like Comb Flower are easier to remember than its botanical name *Micranthus alopecuroides*, we recommend you learn the scientific name. This is because some flowers have two or more common names but only one scientific name. These may change for scientific reasons. In the first edition of this book the Blister Bush was called *Peucedanum galbanum*; it is now called *Notobubon galbanum*. *Gibbaria ilicifolia* has become *Nephrotheca ilicifolia*. Family names can also change.

White-eyed Roella, *Roella ciliata*

Habitat

Under the flower description we provide the likely habitat where each flower is found, such as 'Upper slopes, mainly on the eastern side in good rainfall areas'; 'Lower stony and sandy mountain slopes'; and 'Under trees and damp places on slopes'.

Every plant has a preferred environment in which it thrives. Various factors, like rainfall, altitude, soil type, wind, and the amount of sunshine or shade, determine a plant's habitat (the place where it lives). Generally, the western and northern slopes are fairly dry, while eastern and southeastern slopes and mountain tops are high-rainfall areas.

Maps

Map 1, on the inside front cover, shows the mountain ascents and main hiking paths to be found on Table Mountain.

Map 2, on the inside back cover, shows the mountain ascents and main hiking paths for Silvermine. The major hiking paths on Table Mountain and Silvermine have been colour-coded as follows:

- The Lower Contour Paths are yellow
- The Upper Contour Path is purple (Table Mountain only)
- The ascent routes are green
- The upper slopes' footpaths are orange
- Steep paths from top plateaux to the summits are red

In planning walks, consider the distance of the walk and remember that, in many cases, you will have to make the return trip. Some of the walks can be divided into smaller segments. Be sure to refer to the two maps provided (inside front and back covers) when reading about the walks. For more details about walking on the mountain, see pages 14–25.

Flower-watchers at a ravine overlooking Newlands

View of Silvermine from the Noordhoek Circuit

How to find the flowers

The best strategy to maximise the number of flowers you see is to walk along different hiking routes. Visit as many differing habitats as you can: those with kloofs, streams or seeps, open areas, rocky outcrops, sandy areas, high altitudes, low altitudes, the sunny western side and wetter eastern side. In this way, you increase your chances of finding different flowers. Bear in mind that different flowers grow at different times of the year, so repeating the same routes offers different possibilities as the seasons change.

We are confident that, in the flowering season (August to March), you could see 50 to 100 of the flowers featured in this book *in a day*. If you walk frequently to various parts of Table Mountain and Silvermine, you could see most, if not all, of the flowers in this book *in a year*. You will also see other flowers, not just those in this book. Even when hiking on Table Mountain in the worst months of the year for seeing flowers (April to June), Bruce Mackenzie saw over 100 flowering species per month.

Note that fire triggers off growth in many plants – so when looking for flowers, you would be well advised to hunt in areas recently burnt to find 'specials' for your photographic collection. In fact, fire plays an integral role in fynbos and most species are specially adapted to withstand it; some are dependent on it for flowering.

For those interested in hiking, we describe in the following pages the major hiking routes, putting Table Mountain and Silvermine in different sections. Overviews of the walks are described for each area and summarised in the panel at the end of each section.

MAs

Steps leading to the King's Blockhouse above Rhodes Memorial

Flower walks on Table Mountain

The Contour Paths

The Lower Contour Path, marked in yellow on the map, is suitable for anyone who wants an easy mountain walk. It runs three-quarters of the way around the mountain and has three broad sections.

The first section runs in a northeasterly direction along a relatively flat dirt track from Constantia Nek in the south to a forested footpath above Kirstenbosch. This area is not rich in flowers – until recently, it was covered by pine forest. When you reach Kirstenbosch, consider visiting the upper reaches of these world-famous gardens as there is a superb display of **fynbos** in the top section of the garden, including flowers you will not find on Table Mountain.

From Kirstenbosch, the Contour Path continues – with one short ascent – round the base of Devil's Peak, along an indigenous forest path with boardwalks until you come to a stile just below the King's Blockhouse and above Rhodes Memorial. The path is shady and cool in summer. This is a section of enchanting beauty, with many shade-loving plants and natural forest. The forest itself is not rich in flowers, but as you leave the forest you will come across flowers that enjoy this good rainfall area. Around Rhodes Memorial, in a somewhat grassy open area, you can see pelargoniums, irises and daisies.

The second section of the Contour Path leads around Devil's Peak and across to the northern side of the mountain, ending at Kloof Nek corner. From the stile, the options are either to continue along the 'yellow route' – a dirt road that becomes a tar road running the length of the mountain front and going past the Cable Station – or to take the higher 'purple route'. This runs parallel to the lower road, but about 180 m above it.

This rich flower area was burnt rather badly in January 2006, triggering off an extraordinary display of yellow moraeas, as well as mass displays of purple watsonias. This particular slope of the mountain basks in full sunshine and has few trees, except for a number of cork oaks growing just below Woodstock Cave.

The third section starts at Kloof Nek corner opposite the parking area. Called the Pipe Track, it runs along the western, drier side of the mountain below buttresses known as the Twelve Apostles. This is a rewarding area in terms of wild flowers. In the height of summer, brilliant purple-pink pelargoniums splash the mountainside with colour, and the first part of the track also hosts an annual display of the bright yellow conebush (*Leucospermum conocarpodendron*).

THE LOWER CONTOUR PATH (marked in yellow on Map 1)

Starting point	Description of route
Constantia Nek	**Constantia Nek to the stile below the King's Blockhouse:** From the entrance to the national park at Constantia Nek, follow the dirt road and take the first fork left. Follow this. **Do not** take any further turns. This path eventually becomes a well-marked footpath that runs above Kirstenbosch Gardens. Follow this path, through indigenous forest, to the stile below the King's Blockhouse, above Rhodes Memorial.
Rhodes Memorial	**The stile below the King's Blockhouse to Kloof Nek corner:** Climb up from Rhodes Memorial to the stile below the King's Blockhouse. Go through the stile and walk down the dirt road **(do not** go up to the blockhouse). This road takes you around Devil's Peak to the front of the mountain. It becomes a tarred road, Tafelberg Road, that runs past the Cable Station to Kloof Nek corner. This route is treeless and sunny. *See the purple route on the map for an alternative to road walking.*
Kloof Nek corner	**Kloof Nek corner to Oudekraal Ravine via the Pipe Track:** At Kloof Nek corner there is a Table Mountain National Parks information office where you can find out the starting point of the Pipe Track. Follow this track southwards as far as you want to go. This footpath continues to the bottom of Oudekraal Ravine, where it turns upwards.

THE UPPER CONTOUR PATH (marked in purple on Map 1)

Starting point	Description of route
Rhodes Memorial	**The stile below the King's Blockhouse to Kloof Nek corner – alternative route:** Climb up from Rhodes Memorial to the stile below the King's Blockhouse. Go through the stile and walk up the dirt road to the blockhouse. Just above the blockhouse, to your right, you will find a contour path. Follow this. **(Do not take the path that goes straight up.)** This Upper Contour footpath runs parallel to Tafelberg Road but is higher than the Lower Contour Path. It ends at the entrance to Kloof Nek Waterworks, just above Kloof Nek corner.

The upper slopes

Once up the mountain, the main routes are the Apostles Path (west), Smuts Track (east), the paths around the dams (centre), and those towards the Front Table. All of these paths are marked in orange on Map 1.

The Back Table, about 750 m above sea level, is crisscrossed with numerous footpaths, and many hiking routes are possible as described in the box below. This large area encompasses a wide variety of habitats – wet south-facing rock faces, flat damp areas alongside the dams, flat rocky outcrops, bushy areas and dry open slopes – each habitat supporting particular flowering plants, including proteas, disas, ericas, daisies and irises.

THE BACK TABLE (marked in orange on Map 1) Four major routes are illustrated on the lower Back Table.	
Eastern side of mountain	**Smuts Track** (and/or its extension): This runs from the hiking trail huts just before De Villiers Dam to Maclear's Beacon in the north.
Western side of mountain	**Apostles Path**: This runs from Platteklip Gorge in the north to Grootkop, Judas Peak and Suikerbossie in the south. This is the drier side of the mountain.
The dams	**Back Table**: An easy way to see all the dams is to walk up the Bridle Path and follow it past De Villiers, Alexandra and Victoria dams to the main dams, Woodhead and Hely-Hutchinson.
Between the dams and the Front Table	**Back Table to Front Table**: There are a number of linking paths on the western, central or eastern sides, between the dams and the Front Table. These are clearly shown on the map.

Tree Pincushion, *Leucospermum cordifolium*   Common Sugarbush, *Protea repens*

SA

Scenic view from the top of Table Mountain

The Top Table and the summits

The simplest and quickest way to get to the top of the mountain is by cable car, but you won't see any of the lower-altitude flowers that way. There are 13 fairly commonly used ascents to the top of the mountain. They require a moderate degree of fitness. Always stick to the clear, easily recognisable paths. Once at the top, you have a wide variety of routes along which to explore in search of flowers.

Altitude has an impact on the flowers that grow here. High up, the weather can be harsh: it is colder, wetter and much windier than on the more protected lower slopes and, as a result, the plants on the Front Table are mainly tough, wiry-stemmed reeds, with relatively few flowering shrubs visible. Although there are some lovely flowers on the Top Table (paths marked in red), flower-spotters will see more by walking down to the lower areas, such as the Back Table (orange areas) or the more sheltered lower slopes (yellow areas).

MOUNTAIN TOPS (marked in red on Map 1)

The walks on the higher reaches of Table Mountain and the ascents of Devil's Peak, Grootkop and Lion's Head are shown in red. While the highest peaks have superb views, their climate does not support a huge variety of plants and we recommend the Back Table or lower routes for flower-spotting.

The ascents

The various ascents, usually via gorges or ravines, are described in the table below. These ascents provide shadier, cooler and more sheltered habitats; they are often forested and punctuated by streams.

THE ASCENTS (marked in green on Map 1) (The ascents marked in italics are not recommended unless you know the mountain well or have a good map or guide.)	
Starting point	**Description of route**
1. Constantia Nek	**Bridle Path:** Start at the entrance to the national park. Follow the dirt road. Take the first fork left and next sharp left turn. Thereafter follow this road past an iron bridge to the dams on the Back Table.
2. Cecilia Forest	**Spilhaus Ravine:** Start at the parking spot. Go up the dirt road. Turn first right. Walk straight along here, ignoring a left turn, until you come to a pathway next to a stream that may or may not have water. Go left and up this path. It crosses a dirt road at a hairpin corner and continues upwards. Follow it upwards until it joins the Constantia Nek route.
3. Kirstenbosch Gardens (Rycroft Gate)	**Nursery Ravine:** Start at the Kirstenbosch Gardens' top gate. Follow the brick-paved road through the gardens to the Contour Path. The route is well marked. Follow the sign to Nursery Ravine. Hike upwards.
4. Kirstenbosch Gardens (lower gate)	**Skeleton Gorge:** There are a number of footpaths leading from Kirstenbosch Gardens to Skeleton Gorge that are well signposted. Ask at the entrance for directions if in any doubt. There are ladders halfway up the gorge. A very well-used route with easy rock scrambling. Slippery when wet.
5. Newlands Forest Station	**Newlands Ravine:** From the parking area, go up the tarmac path and turn left. Just past the stream, take the footpath upwards and continue until you reach a dirt road. Turn right, and almost immediately take the hairpin bend left. Follow this road until you come to a sign saying 'Contour Path'. Once you reach the Contour Path, turn right. About a kilometre further on, where there is a picnic table, the ascent path is on your left.

6. Saddle Path parking area	**Saddle Path from Tafelberg Road**: To reach this, drive along Tafelberg Road past the Cable Station, and continue past Platteklip Gorge, where there is a hut with a security guard. Drive on for about another kilometre. You will find limited parking on the left, and the start of the ascent is clearly marked. This is a straightforward climb to the saddle between Devil's Peak and Table Mountain.
7. Platteklip parking area	**Platteklip Gorge**: The Platteklip parking area is just over a kilometre from the Cable Station, travelling in the direction of Devil's Peak. The ascent is a straightforward slog to the top. Once at the top, turn left to go to Maclear's Beacon or right to go to the upper Cable Station.
8. Kloof Nek	*Diagonal Route: From the Kloof Nek parking area, take the Pipe Track for a couple of kilometres until you reach the 'Diagonal Route' signboard on your left. Although this route is safe, it is better to do this with someone who knows the way to the top.*
9. Theresa Avenue, Camps Bay	**Kasteelspoort**: There is limited parking between 25 and 27 Theresa Avenue, Camps Bay. This starting point can be used for ascents on the western side of the mountain. Take the road leading up to the Pipe Track. When you meet the Pipe Track, turn left until you come to the 'Kasteelspoort' sign. This is a well-used route.
10. Theresa Avenue, Camps Bay	**Woody Ravine**: As above, but when you reach the Pipe Track, bear right until you come to the 'Woody Ravine' signpost.
11. Theresa Avenue, Camps Bay	**Corridor Ravine**: From Woody Ravine, continue along the path, cross the Slangolie Ravine stream and proceed up through trees and around the buttress until you reach a fork in the path. Take the left turn to begin the ascent.
12. Theresa Avenue, Camps Bay	**Oudekraal Ravine**: From the bottom of Corridor Ravine, continue straight along a winding path for about a kilometre until the path turns left and starts ascending. This path is not well maintained.
13. Suikerbossie	*Llandudno Ravine: Park outside Ruyterplaats, just before turning left to the Suikerbossie Restaurant. The ascent, while safe, is not described here and should only be attempted with someone who knows the way.*

Silvermine reservoir with a mass of *Erica hirtiflora* in foreground

Flower walks on Silvermine

There are two separate parts to the Silvermine Nature Reserve section of the Table Mountain National Park (TMNP): Silvermine East and Silvermine West. The dividing line is the Ou Kaapse Weg, which provides easy access to this plateau.

The eastern side of Silvermine has superb views of the False Bay coast from many vantage points. In summer the area becomes a kaleidoscope of colour with bright yellow flowers from various Aspalathus bushes, pink Ericas in abundance, the blue shrub *Psoralea pinnata* and the pink-flowered tree *Virgilia oroboides* lining streams, while the white-flowered *Syncarpha vestita* creates snow-like patches in many areas.

The western side of Silvermine provides hikers with stunning views of the Atlantic coast, especially from the higher peaks. In summer, the southern slopes of Constantiaberg can turn white when *Erica lutea* and *Erica mammosa* (the white forms) are in full bloom, while in spring the area glows bright yellow with the Sickleleaf Conebush *Leucadendron xanthoconus* and its eastern slopes showcase the bright pink *Erica abietina* subsp. *constantiana*.

On the map on the inside back cover, we indicate some of the more popular routes in orange. Other easy hiking routes are shown in brown. The access routes that do not start from the Ou Kaapse Weg access points but climb up to the plateau from lower starting points are shown in green. The high peaks or steep, high climbs are shown in red. The yellow sections are generally easily walked, lower contour paths. These routes are just a small section of the available hiking paths.

Entry times for the Ou Kaapse Weg access are:
07:00 to 18:00 (exit by 19:00) October to March
08:00 to 17:00 (exit by 18:00) April to September
A fee is payable (or produce a Wild Card) for entrance to the Western Plateau (Gate 1).

EASTERN PLATEAU ROUTES (marked in orange on Map 2)	
Starting point	**Description of route**
Gate 2	**Higher Steenberg Peak:** From the parking lot, follow the jeep track in a southeasterly direction, past a large map. Simply follow this jeep track and do not turn right at any intersection. The track turns left, going north, shortly after Junction Pool. At the next intersection turn left onto a footpath. Follow this to the peak (537 m), then continue westwards and down a stepped path to get back to the jeep track at the map.
Gate 2	**Two Pools Circuit:** From the parking lot, go past a large map. Stick to the jeep track, keeping left. When you reach the second intersection, Junction Pool is ahead of you, on your right (it dries up in summer). At this second intersection, turn right to go south. You will pass Nellie's Pool on your left. Continue for a short distance until you come to an information hub. Turn right and follow the track which takes you back to the entrance.
Gate 2	**Amphitheatre and Kalk Bay Peak:** From the parking lot, follow the jeep track in a southeasterly direction, past a large map. At the first intersection, turn right and as soon as you have crossed the river turn left onto a footpath (brown on the map). This joins a jeep track where you should go left. A short distance further turn right onto a path that takes you south to the amphitheatre. Stick left at the intersection and follow the path to Kalk Bay Peak (516 m) and a second beacon where there are superb views over False Bay. A descent followed by a more level path brings you back to the jeep track. Turn left and follow this to your starting point.

Xiphotheca fruticosa in the foreground with the Silvermine Reservoir and the southern Peninsula behind

Starting point	Description of route
Gate 1	**The River Walk:** From just inside the entrance parking area, follow the path, which is shady and cool in summer and has boardwalks in places, until it reaches the reservoir. This can be done in reverse. The return trip can be a walk along the road unless a second car is used.
Silvermine Dam parking area	**Elephant's Eye and Constantiaberg:** Start at the reservoir parking area. Follow the jeep track to the right of the dam, staying left at the first junction. Continue up a winding road. At the top of the rise, take the path to the right. Before you reach the Tokai Fire Lookout turn left. Higher up take a path to the right to go to Elephant's Eye Cave, or continue left to the top of Constantiaberg (928 m) where there are superb views in all directions. Your return path starts near the south-westerly corner of the fence around the mast. It takes you to the top of Blackburn Ravine. Turn left here and follow the footpath which joins the jeep track returning you to the start.
Silvermine Dam parking area	**Noordhoek Circuit:** An easy walk along the jeep track, with excellent views from Noordhoek Peak. From the parking area, walk below the dam wall and keep on this jeep track. When you are near the peak, turn left into a short path leading to the summit. Be careful in strong wind. Return to the jeep track and continue your clockwise circuit until you reach a fork in the track. Take the right-hand path back to your car.
East Fort parking area	**Chapman's Peak:** An interesting walk up Chapman's Peak starts at the East Fort parking area and follows the jeep track into Blackburn's Ravine. Cross the river and follow the path south. This path climbs for a while then traverses the slopes below the rock band and eventually arrives at the neck between Chapman's Peak and Noordhoek Peak. At the path intersection go straight (or if you prefer you could take the path to the right which would bring you down to the road where you might have left a second vehicle). You will skirt Lower Chapman's Peak and then climb up to Chapman's Peak (593 m) for superb views all around. Return the same way.

THE ASCENTS (marked in green on Map 2)

Starting point	Description of route
1. Boyes Drive (northern end)	**Steenberg Plateau:** From TMNP map and 'Steenberg Plateau' sign, follow steep path to the top. Go left to Muizenberg Peak or straight to jeep track. From that point there are various options.
2. Boyes Drive (Muizenberg)	**Pecks Valley:** Start at an opening in the stone wall. Ascend to the contour path, turn right, and continue to the top of the plateau. At the junction, go right to Muizenberg Peak (507 m) or left towards St James Peak (422 m).
3. Boyes Drive (just past Muizenberg going south)	**Bailey's Kloof:** Park near Shark Spotters' shelter. Go straight up. Turn right partway up, then left. At the intersection on top go right to ascend St James Peak or straight for Mimetes Valley.
4. Boyes Drive (at 'S' bend where there is a TMNP sign 'Oukraal')	**Old Mule Path and Spes Bona:** Go left along ascending path; at the junction, turn right and follow jeep track. At next junction turn left up slope towards indigenous forest. At head of the valley turn left for the Amphitheatre or right for Kalk Bay Peak.
5. Boyes Drive (southern end)	**Echo Valley:** Ascend without turning off path. Upper end of valley is home to the indigenous Amazon Forest. At the top turn right for the Amphitheatre, or continue around Klein-Tuinkop.
6. Ou Kaapse Weg (southern end)	**Old Wagon Road:** Park in the parking area ±400 m from the Silvermine intersection and follow a jeep track up to the parking lot at the entrance to the reserve (western side).
7. Chapman's Peak Drive (East Fort parking)	**Blackburn Ravine:** Head up past the old fort and zigzag along the jeep track. Near Blackburn Kloof take the upper fork. Cross the river a bit higher up the slope. Follow the path to the top.
8. Chapman's Peak Drive (near top)	**Chapman's Peak:** The path starts beyond the toll plaza (driving south) at a left-hand parking loop. Go uphill. When you reach the intersection you have three choices. Turning right takes you to Chapman's Peak. Turning left takes you to Blackburn Ravine and down to the road. Going straight will take you up to Silvermine, a long, steep climb.
9. Arboretum parking lot (behind Manor House, Tokai Rd)	**Elephant's Eye:** Start at the Arboretum parking lot and follow the path to Elephant's Eye. It is well signposted. You will cross several jeep tracks en route. Where the path levels out, turn right to head for the Lookout and Elephant's Eye Cave.

SAFETY ON THE MOUNTAIN

Beautiful and wondrous as Table Mountain is, it can be hazardous for hikers and should always be regarded with caution and respect. Weather conditions, in particular, can change remarkably quickly. **Every year people have to be rescued, and some die, because they set out inadequately prepared.** Here's a short list of some essential precautions:

- **choose a route that is well marked or that you know well**
- **tell someone where you are going**
- **don't walk alone – for security reasons (muggings have occurred on the mountain) and in case of an accident**
- **carry plenty of water and some nutritious snack food**
- **always wear appropriate footwear**
- **apply sunscreen, even on cloudy days**
- **wear a hat**
- **carry a waterproof jacket and a jersey in your backpack**
- **take a fully charged mobile phone with you (although be aware that certain areas on the mountain do not have mobile phone reception)**
- **take a whistle, small torch and basic first-aid kit**
- **keep to the footpaths and don't take short cuts**

When taking photographs, ensure that you have solid support and be careful of the ground underfoot. It is easy to slip on gravelly stones or wet rock.

Note: *The maps in this book are a general guide. For greater detail, Slingsby's 'Table Mountain' and 'Silvermine and Hout Bay' maps are recommended. They are the only maps of these areas that are endorsed by the Table Mountain National Park, and approved by the Mountain Club of South Africa.*

USEFUL TELEPHONE NUMBERS

SA Weather Office – weather forecast	082 231 1640
Cable Station	021 424 8181
Metro Rescue – medical, rescue	021 937 0300
Mountain Emergencies – security, etc.	086 110 6417
Mountain Rescue	021 948 9900
Orange Kloof permits	021 422 1601

(For Orange Kloof, parties must be accompanied by a volunteer guide. Parties may not exceed 12 people.)

RIGHT: A group of hikers on the Saddle Path

Jan–Dec | Up to 1 m

Wild Aster
Wilde-astertjie
Felicia aethiopica
(Daisy family – Asteraceae)

A leafy, spreading shrub with a hairy flower stem.
Leaves: Thin, lance-shaped, often bent slightly downwards.
Flower head: Single bright blue flower with yellow centre, borne on a long, leafless flower stem. Often found in mass displays.
Distribution: Fairly common.
Habitat: Upper and lower slopes, in bushy and rocky places.

Jun–Sep | Up to 1.2 m

Turquoise Bush Bugloss
Lobostemon montanus
(Forget-me-not family – Boraginaceae)

A large, erect, broad, sturdy, branching shrub.
Leaves: Silvery green, oval to oblong, hairy, stalkless. Leaves widen towards the tip.
Flower head: Blue or turquoise flowers, hairy outside, borne in a large **inflorescence** at the top of the shrub. Has thin 'feelers' (**stamens**) that stick out from the ends of the flowers.
Distribution: Fairly common.
Habitat: Lower sandstone slopes in bushy areas.

Sep–Jan | Up to 15 cm

Fringed Aristea
Maagbossie
Aristea africana
(Iris family – Iridaceae)

A small evergreen **perennial**, often growing in clumps.
Leaves: Thin and narrow, pointed, somewhat sword-shaped.
Flower head: Low-growing, 6-petalled, bright blue, short-lived flowers; 3 yellow **stamens** clearly visible. Each flower lasts a day.
Distribution: Fairly common.
Habitat: Sandy slopes and plateaux.

Pine-leaved Lobelia

Lobelia pinifolia
(Bellflower family – Campanulaceae)

A semi-erect shrublet with leaves that run up the stem to the flower head.
Leaves: Closely packed, overlapping, pine-like.
Flower head: Blue or purple flowers with 5 petals, 3 larger ones below, 2 small above, with 2 sets of white-haired anthers clearly seen (like mini 'tusks').
Distribution: Frequently found.
Habitat: Found among rocks and bushes, often bordering on footpaths.
Notes: The flower head of *L. coronopifolia* is somewhat similar, but that flower has a long bare stem.

| Up to 50 cm | Jan–Dec |

Blue Satinflower

Blousysie
Geissorhiza aspera
(Iris family – Iridaceae)

A tiny, neat, attractive flower with a wiry stem.
Leaves: Light green, long, thin, pointed, partly **sheathing** the flowering stem.
Flower head: Bright blue to violet (sometimes white) cup-like flowers with 6 glossy petals. Flowers grow as a string, all borne to one side, on short stalks towards stem tip.
Distribution: Common.
Habitat: Upper and lower slopes.

| Up to 35 cm | Sep–Dec |

Comb Flower

Vleiblommetjie
Micranthus alopecuroides
(Iris family – Iridaceae)

An appealing, erect herb (**geophyte**) with a comb-like stem.
Leaves: Long, flat, thin, pointed, with an easily seen mid-vein.
Flower head: Tiny pale to dark blue flowers tipped with red, closely packed together; occur in 2 rows up the stem.
Distribution: Rare – found only in a few locations.
Habitat: Sandy places.

| Up to 45 cm | Oct–Jan |

GN

Feb–Apr | Up to 60 cm

Blue Disa
Bloumoederkappie
Disa graminifolia
(Orchid family – Orchidaceae)

A beautiful, slender-stemmed, erect, **tuberous perennial**.
Leaves: Narrow, grasslike, **basal**, that wither and go brown at time of flowering.
Flower head: Attractive, sweet-scented, violet-purple flower, with large upper hood, 2 side petals and, at front, 'Ouma's tongue'. Within the hood, inner petals are tipped with green.
Distribution: Fairly common.
Habitat: Upper slopes, peaks and summits, among **fynbos** and reeds in dry sunny areas.

CM

Oct–Nov | Up to 1.5 m

Blue Sceptre
Blouvuurpyl
Aristea capitata
(Iris family – Iridaceae)

A good-looking, tall, robust plant with a rounded stem and short branches.
Leaves: Long, broad, **strap-like**, sword-shaped, evergreen.
Flower head: Dense **inflorescence** of blue saucer-shaped flowers, crowded together and overlapping, that appear on tall **spikes**.
Distribution: Common.
Habitat: Upper and lower slopes.

MB

Jul–Oct | Up to 1.2 m

Smooth-leaved Bush Bugloss
Lobostemon glaucophyllus
(Forget-me-not family – Boraginaceae)

A common, large, erect and branching shrub.
Leaves: Grey-green, almost entirely smooth, stalkless, lance-shaped leaves that vary in size.
Flower head: Pink or blue flowers, funnel-shaped and hairless outside, in short clusters at the branch tips.
Distribution: Common.
Habitat: Mainly western side, sandy slopes.

Agapanthus
Bloulelie
Agapanthus africanus
(Agapanthus family – Agapanthaceae)

An erect, long-stemmed evergreen **perennial**; flowers in a large cluster, facing outwards.
Leaves: Long, leathery, **strap-shaped, basal**.
Flower head: Large, blue, funnel-shaped flowers, 12–30 in clusters at tip of main stem. A dark blue stripe runs down the centre of each petal.
Distribution: Fairly common.
Habitat: Upper slopes, usually in rocky areas.
Notes: Flowers especially after fires.

Up to 70 cm | Nov–Apr

Blue Pimpernel
Blouselblommetjie
Anagallis arvenis
(Primrose family – Primulaceae)

A small, blue-flowered plant found individually or in small clumps.
Leaves: Stalkless, well-veined, oval-pointed, spaced out on the flower stalk, in pairs, alternately opposite each other.
Flower head: Dark blue (more rarely, red) 5-petalled flower with red centre. Occurs usually at top of long flower stalk.
Distribution: Occasional.
Habitat: Lower slopes, moist areas, well-drained soils. Prefers shade.
Notes: Not indigenous, introduced from Europe. A red form occurs at Suikerbossie.

Up to 40 cm | Oct–Jan

Babiana
Klein-bobbejaantjie
Babiana villosula
(Iris family – Iridaceae)

A dwarf **geophyte** with a deep-seated food store (corm).
Leaves: Hairy, lance-shaped, slender, floppy and longer than the flowering stem.
Flower head: Lightly scented, blue, mauve or violet flower with white centre. Petals are short, hairy, pleated and arranged fan-wise.
Distribution: Fairly common.
Habitat: Mainly lower sandy slopes.

Up to 15 cm | May–Jul

Aug–Jan | Up to 1 m

Blue Rocket Bugloss
Disselblaarluibos
Lobostemon argenteus
(Forget-me-not family – Boraginaceae)

A small, upright, bristly shrublet.
Leaves: Stalkless, silvery green, lance-shaped, partly hairy, with leaf edges curving under.
Flower head: Bright blue, funnel-shaped, with 5 'petals' and noticeably reddish **stamens**. Easily recognised by its upright **spike** from which flowers emerge at top and sides.
Distribution: Fairly common.
Habitat: Mainly drier, sandstone slopes.

Oct–Feb | Up to 50 cm

Golden Disa
Disa cornuta
(Orchid family – Orchidaceae)

A sturdy, upright or semi-erect **tuberous perennial**.
Leaves: Large, broad, overlapping, pointed, tapering in size from the bottom up; streaked with red blotches, they **sheathe** the stem.
Flower head: Unusually attractive, multi-flowered **spike** with distinctive colouring: each flower has a purple-mauve hood, white inside with a purple-black centre spot.
Distribution: Rare – found only in a few locations.
Habitat: Upper slopes, among shrubs, in sandy areas, usually in high-rainfall areas.
Notes: Faintly spice-scented. Also nicknamed the 'Inkspot Disa'.

Aug–Sep | Up to 8 cm

Common Babiana
Bobbejaantjie
Babiana ambigua
(Iris family – Iridaceae)

A small, short-stemmed, dwarf **geophyte**.
Leaves: Narrow, ribbed, hairy, oblong to lance-shaped, longer than the flower.
Flower head: Blue (pink, mauve), fragrant, 6-petalled flower with white to cream markings. Flowers vary in size and colour.
Distribution: Occasional.
Habitat: Sandy soil, lower slopes.

Lady's Hand
Blouraaptol
Cyanella hyacinthoides
(Cyanella family – Tecophilaeaceae)

A small, annual **geophyte**.
Leaves: Large, broad, long, pointed, rising from the base.
Flower head: Slightly scented, pale blue (pink or white) flowers, with 6 backward-turned petals: appear alternately from slender stalks, up an erect stem.
Distribution: Fairly common.
Habitat: Mainly on lower, drier slopes.
Notes: The yellow **stamens** represent the lady's 'hand' complete with fingernails.

Up to 50 cm   Oct–Jan

Wild Sage
Bloublomsalie
Salvia africana-caerulea
(Mint family – Lamiaceae)

The first blue sage to flower. The flower shape resembles a parrot's beak.
Leaves: At base, small, opposite, toothed, grey-white underneath. Upper leaves are bigger.
Flower head: Pale blue to mauve hairy flower. Upper petal hooded, lower petal has a white patch with blue spots. Leaves and flowers are spaced up the stem.
Distribution: Common.
Habitat: Upper and lower slopes.
Notes: *S. chamelaeagnea* looks somewhat similar.

Up to 2 m   Sep–Jan

Drip Disa
Disa longicornu
(Orchid family – Orchidaceae)

A seemingly frail, yet attractive, hanging herb (**geophyte**).
Leaves: Basal, narrow, oval-pointed, pale green.
Flower head: All-pale mauve, strikingly beautiful flower that grows in small groups. Each flower on an individual stem. Large hood, streaked by green veins.
Distribution: Rare – found only in a few locations and locally confined.
Habitat: Upper slopes, on damp to dripping, mossy, shady, south-facing rock faces.

Up to 20 cm   Dec–Jan

31

Oct–Mar | Up to 50 cm

White-eyed Roella
Roella ciliata
(Bellflower family – Campanulaceae)

An attractive flower with distinctive markings.
Leaves: Short, narrow, bristly, covering a thick stem.
Flower head: Single, cup-shaped flower with blue petals, dark inner ring, and white eye (at the base of the throat). Often found with others in clumps.
Distribution: Fairly common.
Habitat: Lower dry sandstone slopes.
Notes: *R. triflora* is similar, smaller, with a black eye at the base of the throat.

Sep–Dec | Up to 1 m

Otholobium
Skaapbostee
Otholobium fruticans
(Pea family – Fabaceae)

An attractive, well-branched, bushy shrublet.
Leaves: Narrow, oval-shaped, with hairy edges, tips turned down, tightly clustered in threes.
Flower head: Consists of a lovely combination of many small mauve and white flowers, interspersed with green **bracts**, in a rounded head. Flowers seem to cascade downwards, almost like a tiered wedding cake.
Distribution: Rare – found only in a few locations on Table Mountain and occasionally in Silvermine.
Habitat: Lower slopes, sandy soils.

Oct–Jan | Up to 75 cm

Lilac Powderpuff
Pseudoselago spuria
(Sutera family – Scrophulariaceae)

An attractive, erect shrub with many branched flowering stems.
Leaves: Thin, ascending, lance-shaped, toothed; taper in size going up the stem.
Flower head: Tiny mauve flowers occur at the top of thin, strong stems, in a densely packed, flat-topped cluster. The mauve-orange patches are unopened buds.
Distribution: Common.
Habitat: Common amid rocks on mountain slopes.

Bush Blue Pea
Psoralea aculeata
(Pea family – Fabaceae)

An erect, densely branched and leafy aromatic shrub.
Leaves: Many, small, semi-folded, closely packed (in threes), with prickly hook-pointed tips.
Flower head: Violet pea-type flowers, scattered along the upper end of branches, provide a mass display. Each solitary flower on individual tiny branchlet.
Distribution: Fairly common.
Habitat: Upper slopes, often near water.

Up to 2 m | Aug–Nov

Fountain Bush
Fonteinbos
Psoralea pinnata
(Pea family – Fabaceae)

An erect shrub, or small willowy tree, with a fairly barren stem.
Leaves: Ascending, thin and rounded, pine-like.
Flower head: Sweet-scented, lilac-blue and white pea-type flowers emerge, in mass display, between leaves towards tips of branches.
Distribution: Frequently found.
Habitat: Upper mountain slopes, damp areas, near dams, streams or forest margins.

Up to 3 m | Aug–Feb

Purple Powderpuff
Blouaarbossie
Pseudoselago serrata
(Sutera family – Scrophulariaceae)

A handsome, erect, leafy shrublet with a stout stem.
Leaves: Oblong, overlapping, leathery, pointed tips bending backwards, edges slightly toothed with a reddish tinge.
Flower head: Tiny, mauve, tubular flowers, densely packed at the top of the plant in a flat-topped or slightly rounded cluster. The mauve-orange patches are unopened buds.
Distribution: Frequently found.
Habitat: Mainly upper mountain slopes.

Up to 90 cm | Oct–Mar

Aug–Nov | Up to 40 cm

Little Blue Mouth
Bloubekkie
Heliophila africana
(Mustard family – Brassicaceae)

A rather stout, sparsely or densely hairy, sometimes sprawling, annual herb.
Leaves: Leaves lance-shaped, sometimes **lobed**; the lower stalked, the upper stalkless.
Flower head: An exquisite blue or mauve flower with 4 rounded spreading petals, a white centre and bright yellow **stamen**.
Distribution: Common.
Habitat: Found on sandy soils among bushes and rocks.
Notes: Needs warm conditions before the flower will open. Closes again when it gets cold.

Sep–Dec | Up to 50 cm

Dark-eyed Bellflower
Wahlenbergia capensis
(Bellflower family – Campanulaceae)

A roughly hairy, erect annual.
Leaves: Stalkless, elliptical or paddle-shaped, wavy or toothed leaves, mainly towards the base of the stem.
Flower head: Solitary, bowl-shaped, pale blue flower with a darker hairy centre; borne on long stalks that are hairy at the base.
Distribution: Occasional, but when found, often in profusion.
Habitat: Sandstone slopes.

Sep–Feb | Up to 40 cm

Table Mountain Plume Aster
Pluimastertjie
Zyrphelis taxifolia
(Daisy family – Asteraceae)

A slender, sprawling, sparsely hairy shrublet.
Leaves: Small, needle-like, minutely toothed.
Flower head: Solitary, blue to mauve petals with a yellow centre, at the top of a long flower stem.
Distribution: Common.
Habitat: Damp sandstone slopes.

Black-eyed Roella
Roella triflora
(Bellflower family – Campanulaceae)

A scrambling or erect shrublet.
Leaves: Long and narrow, often in tufts; hairy, prickly-toothed on the leaf edges.
Flower head: Single, bell-like flowers – varying from pale blue to deep blue with dark blue-black centres – are borne at the end of a woody stem bristling with many pointed stiff leaves.
Distribution: Common in Silvermine, especially in Silvermine East.
Habitat: On sandy lower slopes mainly from Constantia Nek southwards.
Notes: Double flowers have been observed. Can grow in large clumps.

| Up to 50 cm | Dec–Mar |

Wild Lobelia
Kussinglobelia
Lobelia coronopifolia
(Bellflower family – Campanulaceae)

A tufted, erect **perennial** with a long, bare stem.
Leaves: Basal, tufted, dark green, stalkless, deeply **lobed**; usually hairy.
Flower head: Long-tubed, hairless, usually purple or dark blue flowers grow at the end of long, wiry, leafless stems. Five petals: 3 broader, widening at the front, and 2 smaller ones standing up like small horns. White **anthers** are clearly visible.
Distribution: Common.
Habitat: Dry sandy to stony lower slopes.
Notes: Occasionally pink *L. coronopifolia* flowers are found on Table Mountain and Silvermine.

| Up to 40 cm | Nov–Mar |

Blue Pea, Fountainbush
Bloukeurtjie
Psoralea aphylla
(Pea family – Fabaceae)

An erect, willowy shrub or tree with broom-like branches that tend to hang pendulously when in flower.
Leaves: Almost leafless – tiny, narrow, ascending, egg-shaped to lance-shaped leaves occur only on young branches.
Flower head: Single mauve to deep blue-and-white pea-type flowers, consisting of a broad joined petal with 2 smaller lips of a paler colour, are borne at the end of branches on long drooping stems.
Distribution: Occasional.
Habitat: In marshy places, alongside streams.

| Up to 4 m | Oct–Jan |

Cape Scabious
Koringblom
Scabiosa africana
(Scabious family – Dipsacaceae)

A lovely, tall, branched **perennial**.
Leaves: Large, **basal**, roughly oval-pointed with irregularly toothed edges and prominent mid-vein.
Flower head: Mauve, half-round, disc-shaped flower head consisting of tiny, densely packed flowers. Single flower on each long flower stalk.
Distribution: Common.
Habitat: Mainly eastern slopes in sheltered, bushy areas.
Notes: A lookalike, *S. columbaria*, also appears on the mountain but is white.

Aug–Mar	Up to 1 m

Tree Sweet Pea
Keurtjie
Podalyria calyptrata
(Pea family – Fabaceae)

Large branching shrub/small tree, with prolific mauve-pink flowers.
Leaves: Large, green-grey, **simple**, oval-pointed, with easily seen veins.
Flower head: Large, showy, mauve-pink, pea-type, sweetly scented, 5-petalled flowers crowd the branch tips. Back petal is especially large, rounded and deeply notched, going white towards its base.
Distribution: Fairly common.
Habitat: Mainly lower slopes, often in ravines/damp areas.

Jun–Nov	From 3–5 m

Blue Pea Bush
Blouertjiebos
Amphithalea imbricata
(Pea family – Fabaceae)

A handsome, tall, erect shrub with spreading branches.
Leaves: Soft, shiny, grey-green, distinctly veined, oval to lance-shaped; arranged in overlapping, alternately opposite pairs.
Flower head: Mass of small, mauve to purple-violet flowers that are nestled among leaves towards end of branches.
Distribution: Rare – found only in a few locations.
Habitat: Kloofs, upper slopes, also damp stream banks.

Dec–Jun	Up to 1.8 m

Fleur-de-lys
Blou-uintjie
Moraea tripetala
(Iris family – Iridaceae)

A small, eye-catching flower of varying colour.
Leaves: Single, **basal**, narrow, longer than flower.
Flower head: Unmistakable, blue or purple-violet flower, with 3 propeller-like 'petals', each with small white or yellow triangle; occur singly on an erect flower stalk.
Distribution: Common.
Habitat: Upper and lower mountain slopes and flat areas.

Up to 45 cm   Aug–Jan

Bloodroot
Rooiwortel
Dilatris corymbosa
(Bloodroot family – Haemodoraceae)

An unmistakable, erect, **perennial** herb (**geophyte**).
Leaves: Stiff, long, narrow, sword-shaped, arising from the base of the plant.
Flower head: Large, mauve, densely packed, flat-topped **infloresence** consisting of tiny hairy flowers with 6 pointed petals with red-brown tips. Flower head grows on a hairless, grey stem.
Distribution: Rare – found only in a few locations.
Habitat: Mountain slopes, fairly common in Orange Kloof and occasional in Silvermine.
Notes: *D. pillansii* is similar but has shortish **stamens** nestled within the petals; while *D. corymbosa* has longer stamens that rise just above the petals.

Up to 60 cm   Oct–Jan

Bush Felicia
Bosastertjie
Felicia fruticosa
(Daisy family – Asteraceae)

A rounded, densely branched, bushy shrub.
Leaves: Small, narrow, pointed; sprout from the stem in small tufts. Have slight gland spots.
Flower head: Each flower, borne singly, has blue to mauve petals with a yellow centre. Grows on an almost leafless flower stalk. Masses of flowers can appear on a large bush.
Distribution: Frequently found.
Habitat: Upper and lower slopes in drier areas.

Up to 1 m   Sep–Jan

Everlasting Vygie
Altydvygie
Erepsia anceps
(Ice Plant family – Aizoaceae)

An erect, woody, lightly branched **perennial**.
Leaves: Narrow, curving backwards at the tip, spaced up the stem, in pairs opposite each other.
Flower head: Multi-petalled, pink or magenta, daisy-like flowers with a yellow centre; occur at the end of branches.
Distribution: Frequently found.
Habitat: Widespread. Upper and lower rocky slopes.
Notes: Petals tend to remain open in overcast weather.

| Dec–Apr | Up to 30 cm |

Rough Swordweed
Heuningbos
Corymbium africanum
(Daisy family – Asteraceae)

A tufted **perennial** with a thin, tough stem.
Leaves: Basal, long, thin, narrow, **strap-like**, parallel-veined. Up the stem: small, widely spaced, lance-shaped.
Flower head: Tiny pink (purple or white) flower heads form dense flat, or slightly rounded, clusters at tip of the flower stalks.
Distribution: Fairly common.
Habitat: Sandy slopes.
Notes: Flowers especially well after fires.

| Oct–Jan | Up to 30 cm |

Stonecrop
Crassula pellucida
(Crassula family – Crassulaceae)

A soft, **succulent**, scrambling **perennial**.
Leaves: Small, oval-pointed, in pairs opposite each other; faintly toothed; grow directly from round reddish stem.
Flower head: Small, star-shaped, rose-pink flower with 5 pointed petals that become white in the centre. Several flower clusters grow towards the top of leafy stems.
Distribution: Occasional.
Habitat: Upper slopes in damp areas, such as ravines.

| Oct–Apr | Up to 40 cm |

Sickleleaf Brightfig

Lampranthus falciformis
(Ice Plant family – Aizoaceae)

A large, diffusely spreading, low-growing shrub with reddish stems.
Leaves: Small, green or pale green, sickle-shaped, **succulent** leaves with dark tips, grow in groups close to the flowering stem.
Flower head: Bright magenta-pink flowers with glistening petals and a yellow centre grow, solitary or in threes, often in big clusters.
Distribution: Frequent.
Habitat: On ledges or among rocks on mountains.

| Up to 25 cm | Nov–Feb |

Common Romulea

Rooiknikkertjie

Romulea rosea
(Iris family – Iridaceae)

A small, low-growing **perennial geophyte**, variably coloured.
Leaves: Long, thin, stiff, grass-like with 4 small grooves, much taller than the flower.
Flower head: Light pink to lilac-pink, 6-petalled flower with a pale yellow cup (throat), which is often darkly streaked.
Distribution: Common.
Habitat: Lower slopes, especially more sandy or gravelly areas.

| Up to 40 cm | Jul–Oct |

Purple Senecio

Senecio purpureus
(Daisy family – Asteraceae)

A **perennial** hairy herb with thistle-like flower head.
Leaves: Large, widely spaced, deeply **lobed**, found up the stem.
Flower head: Purple flower, with no 'petals', occurs on a short stalk at top of a long, dark pink flower stem.
Distribution: Occasional.
Habitat: Upper and lower slopes.

| Up to 60 cm | Dec–May |

Aug–Oct — Up to 2 m

September Butterfly Bush
Blouertjieboom
Polygala myrtifolia
(Polygala family – Polygalaceae)

A large, sprawling, evergreen, leafy and prolifically flowering shrub.
Leaves: Variable in shape, some flat and oval, others narrower with edges rolled under.
Flower head: Purple-pink and white flowers, in an elongated display towards branch tips. Oval-shaped petals are whitish pink underneath.
Distribution: Occasional.
Habitat: Rocky slopes, especially in forest areas and near streams.

Jan–Dec — Up to 2 m

Spiny Purple Gorse
Kastybos
Muraltia heisteria
(Polygala family – Polygalaceae)

A loosely upright, prickly shrub with spreading branches.
Leaves: Small, prickly, spine-tipped.
Flower head: Small purple flowers with white side petals, scattered between leaves towards branch tips.
Distribution: Frequently found.
Habitat: Widespread, but mainly on lower slopes.

Sep–Jan — Up to 40 cm

Dainty Butterfly Bush
Polygala garcinii
(Polygala family – Polygalaceae)

A small, weak-stemmed, frail-looking shrub, woody at the base.
Leaves: Thin, narrow, needle-like.
Flower head: Small flowers, occurring up the stem – a pink 'bird' with tufted white face and rounded side petals.
Distribution: Common.
Habitat: Upper and lower slopes.

Polygala

Polygala bracteolata
(Polygala family – Polygalaceae)

A thinly branched, spreading shrub.
Leaves: Narrow, lance-shaped on long flower stalks.
Flower head: Pea-type, purple-pink and white flower with 2 pink wings and a white crested fringe; occurs on long pink flower stalks in crowded clusters towards top ends of branches.
Distribution: Frequently found.
Habitat: Upper and lower slopes.

Up to 1 m   Jul–Dec

Granny Bonnet

Moederkappie
Disperis capensis
(Orchid family – Orchidaceae)

A small, erect orchid (**geophyte**).
Leaves: One or 2; long, narrow, pointed, **basal**; also has a few small pointed leaves that **sheathe** the stem.
Flower head: Solitary, dark pink-red flower with a well-defined hood and 'horns' at the top of a short, slender stem. Shape of flower head from the front looks like a woman's bonnet.
Distribution: Occasional.
Habitat: Upper and lower dampish mountain slopes among thick **fynbos**.
Notes: Pollinated by carpenter bees.

Up to 35 cm   Jun–Aug

Indigofera

Indigofera filifolia
(Pea family – Fabaceae)

A tall, erect, branching shrub.
Leaves: Long, thin, thread-like. Almost leafless except for very young plants.
Flower head: Bright pinkish mauve, pea-like flowers, each with an upright, half-round petal above and 2 small petals below; appear towards the tops of tall, straw-thin, green branchlets.
Distribution: Rare – found only in a few locations.
Habitat: Seen near streams in sheltered areas on southern slopes.

Up to 2 m   Feb–Apr

Sep–Jan | Up to 60 cm

Grand Stringbark
Lachnaea grandiflora
(Daphne family – Thymelaeaceae)

An erect, compact, branching shrub.
Leaves: Thick, pointed, oblong to elliptical leaves –
opposite, in 4 rows, densely overlapping – grow up the
stem, pressed against it.
Flower head: Large, 4-petalled, pink or white flowers,
silky outside with pointed hairs, are borne singly at the
ends of branchlets.
Distribution: Fairly common, confined to a limited area.
Habitat: Mainly found in the south.
Notes: Some flowers grow as high as a metre.

Apr–Nov | Up to 50 cm

Persblom
Amphithalea ericifolia
(Pea family – Fabaceae)

A small, erect shrublet with woody branches, hairy when
young.
Leaves: Stalkless, silky, silvery-grey, hairless or silky hairy
above and below, lance-shaped, leaf edges curling down.
Flower head: Violet or rose-coloured flowers with a dark
violet keel grow in round-headed clusters at the top of
flower **spikes**.
Distribution: Fairly common.
Habitat: Sandy soil among rocks, widespread.
Notes: Flowers especially well after fires.

Jan–Dec | Up to 1.5 m

Cape Fellwort
Vlieëbos
Saltera sarcocolla
(Penaea family – Penaeaceae)

A sparsely branched, hairless shrub with slender stems.
Leaves: Grey-green, broad, rounded, leathery,
alternately opposite, overlapping, sharp-pointed leaves,
often covered with a white waxy bloom.
Flower head: Large, bright pink, sticky, glossy-looking,
tubular flowers with 4 lobes (petals) bending backwards
and reddish **stamens**, borne at the top of a crowded
spike. Each head has about 4 blooms.
Distribution: Common in Silvermine, rarely seen on
Table Mountain.
Habitat: On rocky sandstone slopes.
Notes: Pollinated by Orange-breasted Sunbirds, a species
endemic to **fynbos**.

Peninsula Silky Puff
Diastella divaricata
(Protea family – Proteaceae)

A low, single-stemmed, sprawling shrublet often found in dense stands.
Leaves: Flat, egg-shaped to oblong, round-tipped.
Flower head: Broad, pink flowers with a very short floral tube appear mainly at the ends of branches.
Distribution: Fairly common.
Habitat: Found on Silvermine's sandy plateau and sandstone slopes, especially in the south.
Notes: This is the smallest protea.

Up to 50 cm · · · · · Jan–Dec

Wild Cineraria
Strandblommetjie
Senecio elegans
(Daisy family – Asteraceae)

An annual herb, densely covered with gland-tipped hairs.
Leaves: Variably sized, fleshy, deeply **lobed** or divided leaves, often clammy to the touch.
Flower head: Flowers with purple-pink petals and a yellow centre grow at the top of widely separated stems to form a loosely branched **inflorescence**.
Distribution: Common.
Habitat: Lower mountain slopes.
Notes: The leaves of *S. elegans* can be cooked and eaten like spinach. The plant becomes very **succulent** when near the sea.

Up to 1 m · · · · · Jul–Mar

Nude Heath
Erica nudiflora
(Erica family – Ericaceae)

An erect, densely hairy, tightly-packed to sprawling shrublet which provides copious flowers in season.
Leaves: Leaves are relatively long and hairy.
Flower head: Small, pink to red, tubular to narrowly egg-shaped flowers with protruding **anthers** grow in profusion at the end of short branchlets.
Distribution: Frequent.
Habitat: Mountain slopes.
Notes: The plant is usually very hairy whereas the flowers are smooth and dry.

Up to 30 cm · · · · · Feb–Jun

Sep–Apr   Up to 2 m

Hooded-leaf Pelargonium
Wildemalva
Pelargonium cucullatum
(Geranium family – Geraniaceae)

A robust, densely leafed, well-flowered shrub.
Leaves: Long-stalked, hairy, crumpled-looking, crisp, round to kidney-shaped, edges toothed and sometimes reddish, well-defined veins on underside.
Flower head: 8–12 large, purple-pink flowers with well-veined, overlapping petals, in a cluster. Mildly scented when rubbed.
Distribution: Frequently found.
Habitat: Widespread. Sandy and granite soils.
Notes: A white form of this flower may be found occasionally.

Jul–Oct   Up to 40 cm

Lesser Purple Ragwort
Hongerblom
Senecio arenarius
(Daisy family – Asteraceae)

A small, loosely branched annual with a lightly hairy stem.
Leaves: Deeply toothed or **lobed**, somewhat floppy.
Flower head: Several pink-mauve flowers with yellow centres, loosely clustered at the tips of branches.
Distribution: Fairly common.
Habitat: Lower mountain slopes.

Jan–Dec   Up to 1 m

Hairy-flower Heath
Erica hirtiflora
(Erica family – Ericaceae)

An erect, bushy, branching shrub.
Leaves: Small, ascending, needle-like, crowded, in tufts of 4.
Flower head: Small, mauve-pink, oval, covered with short, soft hairs. Often found in mass display on the mountainside.
Distribution: Common.
Habitat: Particularly common in high-rainfall, damp or marshy areas.
Notes: One of the most common ericas, often covering mountainsides in season.

Sundew
Doublom
Drosera hilaris
(Sundew family – Droseraceae)

An upright to sprawling **perennial** with an unbranched stem.
Leaves: Many, long, narrowly oblong; covered with sticky, glistening, glandular hairs that, like tentacles, entrap small insects. Leaves turn red in the sunlight.
Flower head: Purple-pink (also white) flowers with 5 broad, rounded petals, borne on top of a long, thin, dark red stem.
Distribution: Occasional.
Habitat: Mostly upper slopes, in damp, sheltered areas.
Notes: Flowers open only in sunlight.

Up to 40 cm   Sep–Nov

Purple Watsonia
Suurkanol
Watsonia borbonica
(Iris family – Iridaceae)

A beautiful, tall, sturdy **perennial** with a large flower.
Leaves: Long, bright green, glossy, sword-shaped, tough.
Flower head: Bright purple-pink, mildly scented, funnel-shaped flowers with wide petals flaring out; alternately arranged on a green (often purple) stem. Flowers especially well after fires.
Distribution: Frequently found.
Habitat: Widespread. Prefers open mountain slopes.

Up to 2 m   Oct–Nov

Berry Heath
Erica baccans
(Erica family – Ericaceae)

A large, robust, sturdy, colourful, bushy shrub.
Leaves: Small, linear-shaped, ascending, almost pressing against the stem.
Flower head: Tiny, cup-shaped, rose-pink flowers appear in profusion, on short pink flower stalks, at end of branches. Flowers appear in tightly packed groups of 4.
Distribution: Common.
Habitat: Upper and lower slopes.

Up to 2 m   Jul–Dec

Dec–Aug | Up to 60 cm

Beauty Heath
Erica pulchella
(Erica family – Ericaceae)

A small, bright, attractive shrublet.
Leaves: Green leaves in threes, erect, relatively short.
Flower head: Small, bright, deep pink, bell-like flowers, cluster towards the uppermost ends of slender branches in mass displays.
Distribution: Common, especially in Silvermine and southwards.
Habitat: Lower mountain slopes. Can grow in large colonies.

Nov–Dec | Up to 40 cm

Yellow-throated Inkflower
Persinkblom
Harveya purpurea
(Broomrape family – Orobanchaceae)

An erect, slender, silky-hairy **parasitic** herb.
Leaves: Small, rough, scale-like, pale yellow leaves are scattered along the stem.
Flower head: Pinkish red, with wavy-edged, **lobed** petals and yellow blotches in the throat, grow in clusters of 4–5 blooms on short stalks, at the top of a smooth rounded stem covered with small, rough, scale-like leaves.
Distribution: Fairly common in Silvermine, occasional on Table Mountain.
Habitat: Sandstone slopes in sheltered places
Notes: Turns black when pressed or dried.

Sep–Nov | Up to 40 cm

Red Watsonia
Waspypie, Kannetjie
Watsonia coccinea
(Iris family – Iridaceae)

A short, rarely branched **perennial**.
Leaves: Long, slender, lance-shaped **basal** leaves with a prominent mid-vein.
Flower head: Pink, purple or scarlet tubular flowers.
Anthers violet.
Distribution: Fairly common.
Habitat: Seasonally moist sandstone mountain plateau areas, marshes and seeps.
Notes: Flowers more abundantly after fires.

Narrow-leaved Sorrel
Vingersuring
Oxalis polyphylla
(Oxalis family – Oxalidaceae)

An erect plant with many unbranched stems.
Leaves: Has 3–7 thin parallel-sided leaflets that branch out at the end of leaf stalk, like open fingers.
Flower head: Small, single, pale pink, 5-petalled flower with yellow centre, on pink flower stalk. Petals have yellow undersides.
Distribution: Common.
Habitat: Lower slopes.
Notes: Widely found, often regarded as a weed.

Up to 20 cm — Mar–Jun

Purple Inkflower
Jakaranda-inkblom
Harveya pauciflora
(Broomrape family – Orobanchaceae)

An erect **parasitic** herb with a coarse hairy stem.
Leaves: Virtually leafless.
Flower head: Pink-purple flowers grow from a stout, erect, hairy stem. Plants turn black when touched, bruised or dried, like ink spots.
Distribution: Occasional.
Habitat: Northwestern slopes in sheltered rocky places under shrubs.

Up to 60 cm — Dec–Mar

Waxy Satyr Orchid
Rooi-trewwa
Satyrium carneum
(Orchid family – Orchidaceae)

A beautiful, erect flowering plant on a long, stout, brown stem.
Leaves: Two thick, wide and long, pointed, on the ground; others, smaller, **sheathe** the stem.
Flower head: Large elongated head (like an inverted ice-cream cone) covered in dense cluster of pink to rose-coloured flowers.
Distribution: Seemingly rare on Table Mountain, although abundant in other places.
Habitat: Low sandy slopes, dune-bush vegetation.

Up to 80 cm — Sep–Nov

CM

Oct–Jan | Up to 50 cm

Rose-scented Pelargonium
Kusmalva
Pelargonium capitatum
(Geranium family – Geraniaceae)

A low-growing, sprawling, aromatic shrublet.
Leaves: Wrinkled, heart-shaped, with rough irregular edges; pleasant rose-like scent when rubbed.
Flower head: Up to 20 pink-purple flowers, with deep red blotches, in a tight cluster at the top of a strong hairy stalk. Flower heads seem to 'sit up' as though waiting to be noticed.
Distribution: Fairly common.
Habitat: Mainly lower slopes.
Notes: This pelargonium is cultivated for its rose-scented oil.

CM

Nov–Feb | Up to 60 cm

Christmas Berry
Aambeibossie
Chironia baccifera
(Gentian family – Gentianaceae)

A small, richly flowered, multi-branched shrublet.
Leaves: Small, thin, well-spaced and spreading, growing up the stem in pairs opposite each other.
Flower head: Many small, bright pink, 5-petalled flowers scattered around the shrublet.
Distribution: Common.
Habitat: Widespread – likes wind-sheltered and partially shaded areas.
Notes: After flowering around Christmas, small red berries appear, hence its name.

CM/ZG

Jan–Apr | Up to 20 m

Blossom Tree
Keurboom
Virgilia oroboides
(Pea family – Fabaceae)

A tall, profusely flowering large shrub or tree.
Leaves: Many, glossy green above, whitish below; oblong, in pairs opposite each other except for the final leaf.
Flower head: Numerous pale pink or pink-white, sweetly scented, pea-type flowers, closely crowded together; in abundance towards ends of branches.
Distribution: Fairly common.
Habitat: Mainly lower slopes, especially near forest edges and streams.

Darktip Heath

Erica corifolia
(Erica family – Ericaceae)

An erect, hairless shrublet, very variable in terms of its size and floral structure.
Leaves: Green, small, somewhat leathery (*corium* = skin or leather) lie in threes, close to the stem.
Flower head: Urn-shaped flowers, pink below, reddish above, with dark red flower tips, occur on reddish stalks in terminal clusters. The petal tips turn brown soon after the flower opens.
Distribution: Common.
Habitat: Dry sandstone on middle to upper mountain slopes, fewer at high altitudes.

Up to 40 cm Oct–May

Bead Heath

Erica multumbellifera
(Erica family – Ericaceae)

An erect, multi-branched shrub in which everything, apart from the leaves, is reddish.
Leaves: Short, thin and narrow leaves, in **whorls** of 4, rise up the stems.
Flower head: Small, spherical, purple-red flowers grow on a slender stem in bundles, clustered together at the top of branches.
Distribution: Common.
Habitat: Silvermine sandy plateau and in rocky areas.
Notes: Common in Silvermine, rare on Table Mountain.

Up to 50 cm Nov–May

Constantiaberg Heath

Erica abietina subsp. *constantiana*
(Erica family – Ericaceae)

An erect, bushy shrublet with colourful flowers.
Leaves: Green, needle-like, Erica-type leaves (Ericoid).
Flower head: Deep pink, occasionally pale pink, cone-shaped flowers occur in dense clusters along the upper branches.
Distribution: Frequent, seasonally, in specific locations.
Habitat: Mainly found on the slopes of Constantiaberg and Vlakkenberg.
Notes: Brilliant mass displays occur on the eastern slopes of Constantiaberg in season.

Up to 80 cm May–Oct

Sep–Dec   Up to 2 m

Wild Mallow
Kussandroos
Anisodontea scabrosa
(Hibiscus family – Malvaceae)

An erect, indigenous, evergreen, coarse-textured, leafy, aromatic shrub.
Leaves: Rough-textured, somewhat crumpled, sticky, hairy, veined, with deeply cut edges.
Flower head: Fragile, square-looking pink flowers with 5 broad petals, yellow centres and red markings; occur singly, towards branch tips.
Distribution: Rare – found only in a few locations.
Habitat: Lower slopes, sheltered bushy areas on sandy soils. Not found in Silvermine.
Notes: A common garden plant.

Jun–Nov   Up to 45 cm

Hairy-leaved Buchu
Bergboegoe
Agathosma ciliaris
(Citrus family – Rutaceae)

A small, bushy, evergreen shrublet with heath-like foliage.
Leaves: Short, oval, pointed, hairy (hairless with age), aniseed scented.
Flower head: Tiny white or mauve flowers on reddish flower stalks; flowers appear in densely packed, rounded, terminal clusters.
Distribution: Common.
Habitat: Mainly upper slopes.
Notes: *A. ciliata* is similar but less common. Whiter, bigger, with larger, hairy, lance-shaped leaves.

Jan–Mar   Up to 50 cm

Autumn Pipes
Herfspypie
Gladiolus brevifolius
(Iris family – Iridaceae)

A delicate, erect, sometimes scented, **cormous geophyte**.
Leaves: Few, short, **sheathing** the stem, the lowest rust-tipped. Single **basal** leaf appears after flowering.
Flower head: Frail-looking pale pink flower, with 3 upright petals above and 3 narrower ones with yellow spade-like markings below. Often several flowers on stem.
Distribution: Rare on Table Mountain but common further south.
Habitat: Upper slopes, mainly in the south.
Notes: *G. monticola* similar, more apricot in colour, with a more open, bell-like face.

March Lily
Maartlelie
Amaryllis belladonna
(Amaryllis family – Amaryllidaceae)

An attractive, bulbous **geophyte** with a magnificent flower head on a leafless flower stem.
Leaves: Long, **strap-shaped**; appear after flowering occurs.
Flower head: Large, fragrant, pink and white funnel-shaped flowers, each with a golden yellow centre; 6 petals flare widely and backwards.
Distribution: Rare – found only in a few locations.
Habitat: Lower slopes, best after fire.
Notes: Good examples can be seen in Kirstenbosch Gardens.

| Up to 90 cm | Feb–Apr |

King Protea
Koningsuikerbos
Protea cynaroides
(Protea family – Proteaceae)

A large, tall shrub with a magnificent flower head.
Leaves: Large, thick, leathery, somewhat spoon- or paddle-shaped, dark green with reddish edges and long, red leaf stalk.
Flower head: Large, bowl-shaped, creamy white centre, surrounded by long, pointed, greenish yellow or pink to deep crimson spear-shaped 'petals' (**bracts**).
Distribution: Fairly common.
Habitat: Upper slopes, usually in rocky areas.
Notes: South Africa's national flower.

| Up to 3 m | Jan–Dec |

Parasol Lily
Seeroogblom
Crossyne guttata
(Amaryllis family – Amaryllidaceae)

A strikingly unusual bulbous **geophyte** with a large rounded head something like a football.
Leaves: Ground leaves dry and wither at flowering.
Flower head: Round, pink flower head, consisting of tiny reddish brown flowers with 6 small, dark purple, turned-back petals; occurs at end of long pink flower stalks.
Distribution: Rare – found only in a few locations.
Habitat: Lower slopes.
Notes: Flowers only after fires.

| Up to 45 cm | Mar–Apr |

Grand Duchess Sorrel
Grootsuring
Oxalis purpurea
(Oxalis family – Oxalidaceae)

A low-growing **perennial**.
Leaves: Three rounded clover-type leaves, with slightly hairy edges; purplish underneath.
Flower head: Small, deep pink (sometimes white), 5-petalled flower with yellow centre.
Distribution: Fairly common.
Habitat: Lower slopes.
Notes: The white variety is found mainly around the Kloof Nek area.

Jun–Oct	Up to 15 cm

Fish Bean
Tephrosia capensis
(Pea family – Fabaceae)

A low, ground-creeping, straggling **perennial**.
Leaves: Small, narrowly oval-pointed, in pairs opposite each other, like oars in a rowing boat.
Flower head: Deep pink (purple-red), pea-like flowers that can sometimes be seen at the same time as its numerous opaque, hairy seed pods.
Distribution: Fairly common.
Habitat: Lower slopes. Not found in Silvermine.

Jan–Dec	Up to 10 cm

Sissies
Brachysiphon fucatus
(Penaea family – Penaeaceae)

A large, brightly coloured, multi-branched, bushy shrub.
Leaves: Dark green, oval-pointed, growing from the stem.
Flower head: Small, 4-petalled, deep pink, somewhat rectangular flowers appear in a profuse cluster towards the ends of branches.
Distribution: Occasional.
Habitat: Upper slopes and summit areas. Likes cooler, sheltered and shadier areas.

May–Sep	Up to 1 m

Buzz Ixia
Agretjie
Ixia scillaris
(Iris family – Iridaceae)

A pretty, erect **perennial (geophyte)** with a slender stem.
Leaves: Few, long, thin, pointed, with wavy edges, arranged fanwise around the flower stem.
Flower head: Fragrant, 6-petalled, pink flower with bright yellow **anthers.** Flowers face outwards and are spirally arranged up a slim, wiry stem.
Distribution: Occasional.
Habitat: Lower slopes, mainly on the western side, in sandstone and clay areas. Not found in Silvermine.
Notes: Flowers especially well after fires.

| Up to 50 cm | Sep–Nov |

Lessertia
Harslagbossie
Lessertia capensis
(Pea family – Fabaceae)

A small, pretty, ground-hugging shrub.
Leaves: Small, oblong, pointed, occurring in pairs along a trailing stem, with an unpaired leaf at the end.
Flower head: Densely crowded, dark red, pea-type flowers, on short, curved stalks appear at end of long flower stem. Uppermost petal is a lighter pink than the lower ones.
Distribution: Fairly common, less so in the south.
Habitat: Lower rocky slopes, mainly on northeastern to western slopes.

| Up to 10 cm | Aug–Nov |

Cape Sweet Pea
Wilde-ertjie
Dipogon lignosus
(Pea family – Fabaceae)

A small, scrambling shrub that grows on bushes and fallen trees.
Leaves: Dark green, triangular-shaped, blue-grey underneath.
Flower head: Typical pea flower, mainly pink (or purple) with touches of white underneath, growing on a long, slender, twining, woody stem.
Distribution: Fairly common.
Habitat: Lower slopes in forests, forest margins, undergrowth and scrub.

| Up to 2 m | Jul–Jan |

Spider Lily
Spinnekopblom
Ferraria crispa
(Iris family – Iridaceae)

A thick and pulpy flowering plant (**geophyte**) with multi-branched leafy stems.
Leaves: Basal, many, broad, **succulent**, leathery, sword-shaped. Higher up: smaller, overlapping, wrapping round and enfolding each other.
Flower head: Starfish-shaped, variably coloured – from treacle-brown to maroon, to dark purple blotches over yellow or cream. Petal edges wavy, crinkled and crisp.
Distribution: Rare – found only in a few locations.
Habitat: Sandy and rocky areas, lower northeastern slopes.
Notes: Foul-smelling and short-lived; attracts flies.

| Aug–Oct | Up to 80 cm |

Broad-leaved Stork's Bill
Kaneelbol
Pelargonium lobatum
(Geranium family – Geraniaceae)

A long-stalked **geophyte** whose flower shape resembles a windmill.
Leaves: Large – up to 30 cm in diameter, oval-shaped, with ragged edges; lie on ground.
Flower head: Many flowers mass in spreading clusters at tips of flower stalks. Each flower has 5 two-tone petals – dark, purple-black edged with yellow. Clove-scented flowers at night.
Distribution: Occasional.
Habitat: Bushy, sunny areas.
Notes: *P. triste*, very common in Silvermine, has a similar flower head, but the leaves are different – further up the stem, deeply incised, fragmented and feathery.

| Sep–Nov | Up to 50 cm |

Climber's Friend
Steekbossie
Cliffortia ruscifolia
(Rose family – Rosaceae)

A robust, densely branched, prickly shrub.
Leaves: Crowded, dark green, overlapping, lance-shaped, sharply tipped, hairy when young.
Flower head: Small, nondescript red flower found at tips of branches. Has feathery red **stigmas**.
Distribution: Common.
Habitat: Rock faces and ledges, especially in the northern upper areas.
Notes: Strong root system, often used by climbers for support when rock scrambling, hence its common name.

| Jul–Oct | Up to 1.5 m |

Blood Bell Heath

Erica haematocodon
(Erica family – Ericaceae)

A dwarf, straggling, hairy shrublet with twisted and matted branches.
Leaves: Greyish, rough and hairy, glistening, rolled down, in **whorls**. Undersurface white.
Flower head: 1–4 small, dark red, hairy cup- to bell-shaped flowers, with a slightly narrow mouth, grow at the end of short branchlets.
Distribution: Rare.
Habitat: Damp rock faces, usually on south-facing slopes, especially on Constantiaberg and Noordhoek peaks, Silvermine.
Notes: Pollinated by insects.

Up to 30 cm   Nov–Jan

Water Heath

Waterbos

Erica curviflora
(Erica family – Ericaceae)

A large, woody shrub that is often found near water.
Leaves: Fine, hairy, small, linear-shaped, in **whorls** of 4.
Flower head: Many large, hairy, pinkish red curved tubular flowers with trumpet-shaped mouths occur, singly or in pairs, at ends of short, leafy side branchlets.
Distribution: Fairly common.
Habitat: Damp or wet areas: stream banks, seeps, marshes or dry watercourses.

Up to 2 m   Aug–Dec

Summer Snakeflower

Rooibergpypie

Tritoniopsis triticea
(Iris family – Iridaceae)

A brightly coloured summer flower.
Leaves: Basal, long, narrow and pointed. Usually not present at flowering time.
Flower head: Many scarlet, tubular flowers (with 5 curled-back petals) grow alternately at top of unbranched stem.
Distribution: Fairly common.
Habitat: Upper slopes, plateaux and summits, on dry stony ground.
Notes: Pollinated by the Table Mountain Beauty butterfly, *Aeropetes tulbaghia*, which is attracted to red flowers.

Up to 90 cm   Jan–Mar

GN

Mar–Sep | Up to 1.5 m

Coat-hanger Heath
Hangertjie
Erica plukenetii
(Erica family – Ericaceae)

A colourful, tall, erect, bushy shrub.
Leaves: Needle-like, incurved leaves.
Flower head: Large, curved, reddish or white tubular flowers, closely packed together on short **spikes**, emerge towards end of branches and hang downwards. Long brown or yellowish **anthers** protrude beyond end of flower.
Distribution: Frequently found.
Habitat: Widespread, among rocks on dry slopes.
Notes: May flower all year, but mostly March–September.

CM

Jan–Dec | Up to 1.2 m

Tassle Heath
Hangertjie
Erica coccinea
(Erica family – Ericaceae)

An upright, robust and bushy shrub, with short side branches.
Leaves: Short, needle-like, grouped in little tufts up the stem.
Flower head: Bright yellow (or red), slightly curved tubular flowers, with long brown tips, dangle pendulously, in groups of 3, towards ends of branches.
Distribution: Frequently found.
Habitat: Widespread, on dry slopes in rocky areas.
Notes: Yellow form tends to occur in the south.

CM

Jul–Nov | Up to 4 m

Tree Pagoda
Maanhaarstompie
Mimetes fimbriifolius
(Protea family – Proteaceae)

A single-stemmed, wide-spreading, green-leaved shrub or small tree, with cork-like bark.
Leaves: Stalkless, narrowly oblong-shaped with hairy edges; those near flowers are spoon-shaped and dark red.
Flower head: Centred among a mass of yellow-pink 'tongues' reaching upwards. Flowers appear white with wispy, yellow, needle-like **styles**.
Distribution: Occasional on Table Mountain, but fairly common in Silvermine.
Habitat: Mainly the lower plateau, especially misty areas.

Red Disa
Rooi Disa
Disa uniflora
(Orchid family – Orchidaceae)

The largest South African orchid.
Leaves: Long, narrow, bright green, lance-shaped.
Flower head: Beautiful and unmistakable, having 2 wing-like, red petals and a raised upper petal (the hood) that has well-defined scarlet veins.
Distribution: Rare – found only in a few locations.
Habitat: Upper slopes. Permanently wet or moist places, such as beside streams, wet cliff faces and seepage lines.
Notes: Floral emblem of Western Cape. *Disa rosea* is also found at the aqueduct in October.

| Up to 60 cm | Jan–Feb |

Cat's Claws
Katnaels
Hyobanche sanguinea
(Broomrape family – Orobanchaceae)

A leafless, root-**parasite** with a tubular stalk.
Leaves: None.
Flower head: Crimson red or bright pink flowers that look like a clump of hairy and podgy cylindrical fingers.
Distribution: Rare – found only in a few locations.
Habitat: Upper and lower slopes, in sheltered areas under bushes.
Notes: Feeds on the roots of various shrubs, especially daisies.

| Up to 15 cm | Aug–Oct |

Red Crassula
Klipblom
Crassula coccinea
(Crassula family – Crassulaceae)

A colourful, upright **succulent** with a few side branches.
Leaves: Shiny green, broad, oval-pointed; symmetrically arranged around the stem, in overlapping, alternately opposite pairs.
Flower head: Small, bright red-scarlet, fragrant flowers, with 5 curved, pointed petals; occur, densely packed, in a flat-topped **inflorescence**.
Distribution: Frequently found.
Habitat: Mainly upper slopes. Rocky areas, ledges, crevices.
Notes: An albino variation has been recorded in the Kasteelpoort area on Table Mountain.

| Up to 50 cm | Dec–Mar |

Feb–Jun   Up to 90 cm

Wine-rose Heath
Wynpienkheide
Erica abietina subsp. *atrorosea*
(Erica family – Ericaceae)

An erect, bushy shrub with eye-catching flowers.
Leaves: Short and narrow, needle-like, rise up the stem in **whorls**, curving slightly inwards.
Flower head: Reddish-pink, sticky, curved and tubular in shape with a widened mouth and **anthers** extending beyond mouth. Grow towards ends of branches: continuing branch growth occurs above **inflorescence**.
Distribution: Occasional to frequent, depending on location.
Habitat: Lower mountain slopes, mainly from Constantia Nek southwards.
Notes: Found especially in the southeastern section of Silvermine in places exposed to cool breezes of False Bay.

Mar–Apr   Up to 45 cm

Guernsey Lily
Berglelie
Nerine sarniensis
(Amaryllis family – Amaryllidaceae)

An erect, beautiful flower on a long flower stalk.
Leaves: Broad, **strap-shaped**, rounded at tip; appear after flowering.
Flower head: Each large flower contains 6 crimson petals with a golden sheen. Petals flare out and curve backwards.
Distribution: Rare – found only in a few locations.
Habitat: Shady places on rocky slopes.
Notes: A Dutch ship carrying Cape bulbs to Holland was wrecked on Guernsey Island in 1659. The flowers grew and were first described there. It is endemic to the Cape.

Feb–Apr   Up to 45 cm

Cluster Disa
Monnikskappie
Disa ferruginea
(Orchid family – Orchidaceae)

An attractive, **tuberous perennial**.
Leaves: Narrow, long, grass-like, **basal** – appear after flowering. Has small, **sheathing** leaves up the stem.
Flower head: Eye-catching, bright orange-red, open-mouthed flowers crowd in an elongated, loosely formed, often triangular-shaped cluster, on dark red stalk.
Distribution: Common.
Habitat: Upper slopes, usually among bushes and rocks.
Notes: Pollinated by the Table Mountain Beauty butterfly, *Aeropetes tulbaghia*, which is attracted to red flowers.

Common Paintbrush
Veldskoenblaar
Haemanthus sanguineus
(Amaryllis family – Amaryllidaceae)

An erect, fleshy **geophyte** with a stout, unmarked stem.
Leaves: Two, flat, rounded, edged with red, appear after flowering. The previous year's dry brown leaves may be seen.
Flower head: Large, deep red, circular flower head, crammed with tiny, yellow flowers with bright yellow **anthers**, borne at the top of a thick, cylindrical, red stem.
Distribution: Reasonably common.
Habitat: Fairly common on the lower slopes in dampish areas.
Notes: *H. sanguineus* is also called April Fool. *H. coccineus* has a stem that is spotted and barred, and longer leaves.

Up to 30 cm   Feb–Apr

April Fool
Misryblom
Haemanthus coccineus
(Amaryllis family – Amaryllidaceae)

An erect, fleshy **geophyte** with a stout, pale dull green stem marked with red spots or streaks.
Leaves: Two leathery, smooth, broad, tongue-shaped leaves, spreading or erect, appear after flowering.
Flower head: Large red or pink, circular flower head, crammed with tiny yellow flowers with bright yellow **anthers** borne on top of thick, cylindrical stem.
Distribution: Fairly common.
Habitat: On lower rocky slopes, often in large clumps, especially in Silvermine.
Notes: *H. sanguineus* looks similar but has unmarked stem and shorter leaves.

Up to 20 cm   Feb–Apr

Ninepin Heath
Rooiklossieheide
Erica mammosa
(Erica family – Ericaceae)

An erect, colourful shrub with many branches.
Leaves: Short, needle-like, in **whorls** of 4, pressing against the stem.
Flower head: Dark red to pink (purple, orange-red, green-cream) flowers in dense clusters at the end of branches; long flower stalks, flowers hang downwards.
Distribution: Occasional.
Habitat: Widespread. Rocky and sandy seepage areas.

Up to 1.5 m   Dec–Apr

Fire Heath
Rooihaartjie
Erica cerinthoides
(Erica family – Ericaceae)

An erect and compact shrub with a few semi-erect branches.
Leaves: Short, needle-like, grouped in 4s (sometimes more), ascending in **whorls** around the stem.
Flower head: Long, fat, tubular flowers, bright orange-red with tiny, white hairs; sometimes sticky; occur hanging downwards, at the end of branch tips, in a crowded, rounded cluster.
Distribution: Occasional.
Habitat: Upper and lower rocky slopes.
Notes: Especially noticeable after fires.

Jul–May	Up to 1 m

Lesser Cobra Lily
Suurkanolpypie
Chasmanthe aethiopica
(Iris family – Iridaceae)

An erect, **perennial** herb with an unbranched stem.
Leaves: Large, sword-shaped, **basal**, **sheathing** the flower stem.
Flower head: Single row of large, curved, bright orange-red tubular flowers, curving outwards, each with a long, hooded top petal and smaller lower petals. Flower head bends significantly towards the end of its flowering **spike**.
Distribution: Occasional.
Habitat: Under trees and damp places on slopes.
Notes: *C. floribunda* is similar except it is larger, has a branched stem, and a double row of flowers.

Jun–Aug	Up to 65 cm

Ganna Bush
Gonnabos
Passerina corymbosa
(Daphne family – Thymelaeaceae)

A shrub or small tree, having slender white stems when young and covered with leaves.
Leaves: Long and narrow, opposite, narrow, hairy, grooved.
Flower head: Yellow and dull red flowers cluster in an oval **spike** at the end of branches.
Distribution: Common.
Habitat: On sandy, often disturbed slopes, such as roadsides.
Notes: Wind-pollinated. Clouds of pollen erupt when the branch is shaken.

Oct–Nov	Up to 2-3 m

Fire Lily
Brandlelie
Cyrtanthus ventricosus
(Amaryllis family – Amaryllidaceae)

An attractive, sturdy, bulbous **geophyte** with beautiful flowers.
Leaves: Not apparent (dry) at the time of flowering, emerge after the flower has bloomed.
Flower head: Bright red to vermilion tubular flowers, widening towards the mouth, are borne on a brownish maroon **inflorescent** stalk. Some flowers remain erect, others hang pendulously.
Distribution: Locally common after fires between December and May.
Habitat: South-facing sandy mountain slopes.

Up to 20cm | Dec–May

Rat's Tail
Rotstert
Babiana ringens
(Iris family – Iridaceae)

A **geophyte** with a strong, erect, leafless, downy stem, sometimes slightly curved forming a bird-perch for pollinating sunbirds.
Leaves: Narrow, very stiff, hairless or minutely haired, pleated, sharp-tipped.
Flower head: Bright red with a yellow throat, grow in profusion on a short side branch at ground level.
Distribution: Occasional.
Habitat: Sandy soils, usually near the coast.
Notes: The bird-perch is an elongated sterile flower spike that extends 4–5 times the height of flowers, resembling a rat's tail.

Up to 40 cm | Aug–Oct

Rock Heath
Erica nevillei
(Erica family – Ericaceae)

A robust, low-growing, semi-sprawling, rock-scrambling, woody shrublet.
Leaves: Slender spreading leaves, in **whorls** of 5–6.
Flower head: Long, sticky, bright red tubular flowers, slightly curved, grow near the end of branches; the **anthers** protrude beyond the mouth.
Distribution: Uncommon, confined to a limited area.
Habitat: Found on Silvermine's western plateau.
Notes: Endemic: Constantiaberg and Noordhoek mountains; also found on Kalk Bay Peak on the eastern side of Silvermine.

Up to 40 cm | Jan–May

Dec–Jan · Up to 1 m

Pig's Ear
Varkoor
Cotyledon orbiculata
(Crassula family – Crassulaceae)

An erect, evergreen, **succulent**-leaved shrublet with a long flower stem.
Leaves: Thick, waxy, green-grey, rounded but variably shaped, with thin, red, glossy edges.
Flower head: Colourful, bright red-orange, waxy, bell-shaped flowers with 5 curled-back petals hang pendulously in bunches from top of long flower stem.
Distribution: Occasional.
Habitat: Lower slopes, generally on the drier western side, in bushy places, often sandy and rock-strewn.

Jun–Jul · Up to 70 cm

Red Afrikaner
Rooipypie
Gladiolus priorii
(Iris family – Iridaceae)

A striking, yet delicate, erect **perennial** herb (**geophyte**).
Leaves: Long, narrow, pointed; the bottom one completely **sheathes** the stem.
Flower head: Bright red, with 6 oval-pointed petals and a pale yellow patch at the throat. Up to 5 flowers are borne on the unbranched flower stem.
Distribution: Occasional on Table Mountain, but common in Silvermine.
Habitat: Lower, mainly southeastern slopes, among bushes.

Aug–Dec · Up to 1 m

Balloon Pea
Kankerbos
Sutherlandia frutescens
(Pea family – Fabaceae)

A well-branched, erect or sprawling shrub.
Leaves: Grey-green, oblong, rounded at tip, slightly hairy, in pairs opposite each other.
Flower head: Bright orange-red, hanging flowers open at the mouth; large, smooth, inflated, translucent, bladder-like, pale green and reddish brown pods.
Distribution: Occasional.
Habitat: Dry slopes in rocky-sandy areas.
Notes: Called 'Cancer Bush' for its supposed cancer-healing properties.

Red Heath
Rooiklossieheide
Erica abietina subsp. *abietina*
(Erica family – Ericaceae)

An erect, brightly coloured, slightly hairy shrublet.
Leaves: Short, thread-like, splaying out horizontally and curving upwards, rising up the stem.
Flower head: Bright red, shiny, fat, somewhat sticky, curved tubular flowers appear in densely crowded, spreading clusters at branch tips.
Distribution: Frequently found on Table Mountain only.
Habitat: Widespread. All slopes up to the summit. Likes sunny areas.

Up to 1 m — Jan–Dec

Brown-beard Sugarbush
Baardsuikerbos
Protea speciosa
(Protea family – Proteaceae)

A small, erect, multi-stemmed shrub.
Leaves: Thick, leathery, broadly elliptical, pointed.
Flower head: Pale pink and white overlapping 'petals' (**bracts**).
Distribution: Occasional.
Habitat: Mainly upper slopes.
Notes: The only multi-stemmed bearded sugarbush.

Up to 1.2 m — Sep–Oct

Common Sugarbush
Suikerbos
Protea repens
(Protea family – Proteaceae)

A pretty, robust, erect shrub or tree.
Leaves: Narrow, long, pointed, somewhat oblong to spatula-shaped.
Flower head: Distinctive cream to pink, deep pink or red, bicoloured, shaped like an ice-cream cone.
Distribution: Occasional.
Habitat: Varied; lower slopes.
Notes: This was the national flower of South Africa until 1976.

From 3–5 m — May–Oct

GN

Jun–Oct | Up to 8 cm

Yellow-eyed Sorrel
Geeloogsuring
Oxalis obtusa
(Oxalis family – Oxalidaceae)

A tiny, bright and attractive flower.
Leaves: Hairy, divided into 3 heart-shaped leaflets, deeply notched at tips.
Flower head: Small, orange-pink flower with 5 wedge-shaped petals and yellow centre; often found in clumps. Reddish veining on petals.
Distribution: Common.
Habitat: Lower slopes on rock, sand, clay or granite.
Notes: A yellow form is sometimes found on the eastern slopes of Devil's Peak.

GN

Nov–Feb | Up to 1.7 m

Table Mountain Watsonia
Watsonia tabularis
(Iris family – Iridaceae)

A tall, erect, multi-branched flower.
Leaves: Basal, long, flat, broad, sword-shaped. The leaves **sheathe** the stem closely and catch drops of water.
Flower head: Large, tubular, curved, 6-petalled flower, salmon to orange-pink; flowers flare open, funnel-shaped, at the mouth.
Distribution: Frequently found.
Habitat: Upper and lower slopes. Likes moist or marshy places.
Notes: Pollinated by sunbirds. Flowers best after fires.

GN

Jul–Jan | Up to 2 m

Brown Sage
Bruinsalie
Salvia africana-lutea
(Mint family – Lamiaceae)

A densely leafed, loosely spreading shrub.
Leaves: Oval-shaped, pointed, green-grey, aromatic, hairy.
Flower head: Unusual flowers: shaped like a parrot's beak and coloured treacle brown. Flowers in profusion, in pairs at branch tips.
Distribution: Fairly common.
Habitat: Bushy places, often found on sandy soils.
Notes: Early European botanists, looking at dried specimens, named the plant 'lutea' (meaning yellow), in the belief that there were no brown flowers.

Common Butterfly Lily
Rooikanol
Wachendorfia paniculata
(Bloodroot family – Haemodoraceae)

An erect, branching **perennial**.
Leaves: Basal, long, broad, veined, mainly **strap-like**, with an elongated, pointed tip.
Flower head: Multi-branched stem hosts flowers with 6 yellow and brownish petals. Flowers grow and open, alternately, from the bottom of the stem, upwards.
Distribution: Fairly common.
Habitat: Upper and lower mountain slopes, often in sheltered areas.
Notes: Flowers profusely after fires.

Up to 70 cm   Aug–Nov

Wandering Jew
Wandelende Jood
Commelina africana
(Commelina family – Commelinaceae)

A straggling, **perennial** ground cover.
Leaves: Broad, oval-shaped, alternate, strong mid-vein; **sheathe** the flower stem.
Flower head: Yellow-orange flowers with 3 petals, 1 being very small.
Distribution: Fairly common.
Habitat: Among bushes and rocks on lower mountain slopes. Often found near streams.

Up to 50 cm   Jan–Dec

Autumn Painted Lady
Bergpypie
Gladiolus monticola
(Iris family – Iridaceae)

A slender, erect **perennial geophyte**.
Leaves: A single **basal** leaf appears after flowering.
Flower head: Pink to salmon-apricot flower with 6 pointed petals, the lower 3 having a variable yellow stripe outlined by a pink arrow or W-shaped mark. Several flowers may bloom simultaneously on the flower stalk.
Distribution: Common on Table Mountain, but rare in the south.
Habitat: Upper slopes, top plateaux and summits.
Notes: The only gladiolus endemic to the Cape Peninsula.

Up to 70 cm   Jan–Mar

GN

Oct–Mar | Up to 1.3 m

Noughts and Crosses
Penaea mucronata
(Penaea family – Penaeaceae)

An erect, woody, leafy, branching shrub.
Leaves: Thick, smooth, somewhat triangular, growing directly from the reddish stem, tips outwards; arranged in closely ranked, alternately opposite pairs, giving the plant a square look.
Flower head: Four-petalled yellow and red flowers, in a cluster at ends of short **spikes**.
Distribution: Frequently found.
Habitat: Widespread on rocky sandstone slopes.

SM

Nov–Jan | Up to 1.5 m

Wild Dagga
Wildedagga
Leonotis leonurus
(Mint family – Lamiaceae)

A large, tall, erect, unusually shaped, hairy shrub.
Leaves: Narrow, long, lance-shaped, with leaf edges toothed, saw-like, 'teeth' pointing forwards.
Flower head: Orange-coloured flowers, with long, hooded tubes and shorter lower lips, clustered in dense **whorls**, one cluster above the other.
Distribution: Occasional.
Habitat: Lower bushy slopes, in reasonably damp areas.

ZG

Sep–Jan | Up to 1.5 m

Tree Pincushion
Leucospermum cordifolium
(Protea family – Proteaceae)

An attractive, rounded, bushy shrub with beautiful flowers.
Leaves: Somewhat egg/heart-shaped, toothed towards the leaf tips.
Flower head: Large, orange-red to scarlet, rounded, pincushion-type.
Distribution: Only in a few specific locations.
Habitat: Does not occur naturally on mountain.
Notes: Non-indigenous to the Cape Peninsula.

Mountain Dahlia
Bergdahlia
Liparia splendens
(Pea family – Fabaceae)

A brightly coloured, slender-stemmed, fairly rigid, multi-branched shrub.
Leaves: Abundant, overlapping, narrowly oval, well-veined, leathery.
Flower head: Large, orange-yellow-red flower with numerous long, overlapping, pointed petals appear, drooping, in crowded cluster at end of flower stem.
Distribution: Rare on Table Mountain, but fairly common in Silvermine.
Habitat: Grows in the south, on damp mountain slopes.

Up to 1 m — Oct–Jan

Orange Ixia
Oranjekalossie
Ixia dubia
(Iris family – Iridaceae)

A small, bright and colourful flower.
Leaves: Long, narrow, sword-shaped.
Flower head: Bright orange-yellow flower, with 6 oval-pointed petals, sometimes tipped with red, and often with purple or dark brown centre. Petal undersides reddish. Flowers occur at tops of thin, sturdy stems, **sheathed** from the base by long, pointed leaves.
Distribution: Fairly common.
Habitat: Upper and lower slopes, often bordering footpaths; mainly western side of mountain.

Up to 35 cm — Sep–Dec

Grey Tree Pincushion
Kreupelhout
Leucospermum conocarpodendron
(Protea family – Proteaceae)

A large, rounded shrub or tree, with many branches.
Leaves: Wedge-shaped, silver-grey, covered with minute, woolly hairs, red-tipped and toothed towards leaf tips.
Flower head: Bright yellow, pincushion-type flower.
Distribution: Fairly common.
Habitat: Mainly lower slopes, especially in northwest.
Notes: Subspecies *viridum* is similar, has dark green, hairless leaves. It occurs from Kirstenbosch southwards.

From 3–5 m — Aug–Dec

Mar–Aug — Up to 15 cm

Cape Fire Arctotis
Brandblom
Haplocarpa lanata
(Daisy family – Asteraceae)

A large, sun-loving, yellow flower, with crowded leaves at the base of the stem.
Leaves: Somewhat rough, oval-shaped, dark green above, grey-white and hairy underneath, well-veined.
Flower head: Daisy-type flower with yellow petals and centre; petals are red or purple on reverse. Solitary flowers are borne at the end of long, dark red, bare stems.
Distribution: Common.
Habitat: Sunny mountain slopes.
Notes: Especially noticeable after fires.

Aug–Jan — Up to 1 m

Spiny Aspalathus
Aspalathus barbata
(Pea family – Fabaceae)

A robust, leafy shrub with an erect stem and wand-like branches.
Leaves: Lance-shaped, veined, spiny, bending backwards and outwards.
Flower head: Yellow pea-type flowers, turning red with age; nestle in leaves in terminal clusters at top of flower spike.
Distribution: Occasional.
Habitat: Upper slopes, especially after fires.
Notes: *A. cordata* is similar but has larger leaves and flowers.

Jul–Jan — Up to 1 m

Sticky Tar Pea
Teer-ertjie
Bolusafra bituminosa
(Pea family – Fabaceae)

A twining, scrambling, hairy shrub.
Leaves: Dark green, broad, rounded, well-veined, tar-scented when rubbed; consist of 3 leaflets.
Flower head: Bright yellow, pea-type flowers, with red scratch markings on backs of uppermost petals, grow along elongated flower stalks.
Distribution: Fairly common.
Habitat: Cooler bushy places on hillsides, often near streams.
Notes: Especially noticeable after fires.

Thread-leaved Klaas Louw Bush
Klaaslouwbossie
Athanasia crithmifolia
(Daisy family – Asteraceae)

A large, leafy shrub with a firm, upright stem.
Leaves: Many, thin, needle-like, somewhat forked or trident-shaped.
Flower head: Mass of tiny, bright yellow, scented flowers that combine to form a densely packed, flat-topped cluster.
Distribution: Common.
Habitat: Upper and lower slopes, often along drainage lines.
Notes: The flowers emit a strong, sickly-sweet scent.

Up to 1.5 m | Oct–Feb

Yellow-tipped Strawflower
Helichrysum cymosum
(Daisy family – Asteraceae)

One of the most commonly found strawflowers – an erect, easily recognised shrub.
Leaves: Thin, white-felted underneath, leaf edges rolling slightly backwards towards underside.
Flower head: Tiny, bright yellow flowers, densely packed in a compact head, appear at ends of tall, grey flower stems.
Distribution: Frequently found.
Habitat: Widespread, especially on damp slopes.
Notes: Perhaps the most commonly found flower on the mountain, in season.

Up to 1 m | Sep–Apr

Golden Cowcud
Beesbos
Chrysocoma coma-aurea
(Daisy family – Asteraceae)

An easily recognised, erect, leafy shrublet.
Leaves: Small, thin, bending, near horizontal, growing neatly up the stem. Leaf edges curl slightly downwards.
Flower head: Button-like yellow flower, without petals, appears, singly, at tips of slender flower stems. Often found in large clumps.
Distribution: Common.
Habitat: Upper and lower slopes, sunny areas.

Up to 50 cm | Sep–Jan

SM

Rush-leaved Moraea
Geelflappie
Moraea neglecta
(Iris family – Iridaceae)

An erect, unbranched **geophyte**.
Leaves: Single leaf, narrow, channelled, cylindrical.
Flower head: Fragrant, yellow with dark speckled markings.
Distribution: Occasional.
Habitat: Upper and lower slopes of sand, peat or granite.

Sep–Dec | Up to 50 cm

CW

Painted Yellowwort
Naeltjiesblom
Sebaea exacoides
(Gentian family – Gentianaceae)

A small, brightly coloured flower, often found in small clusters.
Leaves: Small, oval-pointed.
Flower head: Five-petalled, flat-headed, bright yellow flower, with 2 short, orange-red parallel lines at base of each petal.
Distribution: Frequently found.
Habitat: Mainly lower slopes in sandy areas.
Notes: The parallel lines are ridged swellings, containing a sweetness that attracts insects.

Jul–Oct | Up to 30 cm

HC

Painted Peacock
Sterretjie
Spiloxene capensis
(Stargrass family – Hypoxidaceae)

A small, erect, attractive flower with many colour forms.
Leaves: Long, thin, pointed, needle-like, **sheathing** the flower stem at the base.
Flower head: Single, star-shaped, white, yellow, rarely pink, with 6 tapering petals; centre and petal tips often dark red.
Distribution: Common.
Habitat: Mainly upper slopes, seasonally wet areas.
Notes: The lookalike yellow *Empodium plicatum* flowers in winter (April–June).

Aug–Oct | Up to 30 cm

Heart-leaved Gorse
Steekertjiebos
Aspalathus cordata
(Pea family – Fabaceae)

An upright, robust, well-branched shrub.
Leaves: Large, prickly pointed, growing out from sides of stem, as though with cupped hands to gather water.
Flower head: Bright, yellow, pea-like flowers in terminal cluster at end of branches. Flowers go bright orange with age.
Distribution: Fairly common.
Habitat: Lower stony slopes.
Notes: *A. barbata* is similar but has more leaves and smaller flowers.

Up to 1 m   Sep–Jan

Holly-leaved Wild Thistle
Berkheya barbata
(Daisy family – Asteraceae)

An erect, rigid, spiny shrublet with greyish branches.
Leaves: Broad, green, leathery with thorny edges, white-felted underneath; in pairs, alternately opposite each other.
Flower head: Solitary, large, yellow daisy flower, with thin, square-tipped 'petals', occurs at end of branch tips.
Distribution: Occasional.
Habitat: Rocky sandstone slopes.

Up to 60 cm   Sep–Dec

Sprawling Bush Thistle
Steekhaarbos
Cullumia setosa
(Daisy family – Asteraceae)

A robust, prickly, sprawling, leafy shrublet.
Leaves: Oval, bending backwards, leaf tips sharply pointed, hook-like.
Flower head: Single yellow flower at top of bristly, intertwining branches.
Distribution: Common.
Habitat: Upper and lower slopes.

Up to 60 cm   Jul–Dec

Common Honeybush
Heuning tee
Cyclopia genistoides
(Pea family – Fabaceae)

An erect, robust, profusely branched shrub with tan-brown stem and clusters of bright flowers.
Leaves: Dull green leaves, each with 3 narrow (finger-like) leaflets with rolled-under leaf edges.
Flower head: The bright yellow, pea-like flowers grow in showy clusters at the tips of branches.
Distribution: Frequent.
Habitat: Lower slopes in seasonally marshy and damp areas and sandy areas.

Jul–Dec   Up to 2m

Golden Head Cape Gorse
Aspalathus callosa
(Pea family – Fabaceae)

An erect, bright green shrublet with upward-curving branches.
Leaves: Long and narrow leaflets in threes; hairless, flat, fleshy, needle-like.
Flower head: Bright yellow flowers appear in neat, rounded to egg-shaped flower clusters at the end of upright branches.
Distribution: Fairly common.
Habitat: On sandy lower slopes.

Oct–Dec   Up to 60 cm

Lesser Reedpipe
Pepersouskousie
Tritoniopsis parviflora
(Iris family – Iridaceae)

An erect, slender **geophyte**.
Leaves: Long, slender, 1–2-veined **basal** leaves, narrow then widening, which emerge before flowering, brown at time of flowering.
Flower head: Pepper-scented, small, short-tubular yellow flowers with brown to maroon markings; 2 ear-like petals and 3 smaller wavy lobes, spirally arranged in a dense display at the top of a rounded stem.
Distribution: Fairly common.
Habitat: Rocky sandstone slopes; damp, sandy, marshy places on Silvermine plateau and mountain slopes.

Nov–Feb   Up to 40 cm

Fivetooth Baboon Cabbage

Bobbejaankool

Othonna quinquedentata

(Daisy family – Asteraceae)

A single-stemmed, erect shrub with several slender, branching stems.

Leaves: Smooth, hairless, slightly fleshy, wedge-shaped to lance-shaped leaves, often edged or spotted in red and toothed in the upper part, occur on the lower stems.

Flower head: Small yellow flowers with neat, rounded petals, set in a small green cup on a short flower stalk, grow on almost leafless branched stems in loosely branched **inflorescences**.

Distribution: Common.

Habitat: On mountain slopes, often in damp places.

Up to 2.0 m   Oct–Jul

Hairystalk Boneseed

Osteospermum polygaloides

(Daisy family – Asteraceae)

An erect, small shrublet.

Leaves: Blue-green, stalkless, leathery, oblong to oval leaves; tips hooked.

Flower head: Single yellow flowers are borne on a long, rough-hairy stalk.

Distribution: Frequent.

Habitat: At low altitudes, mainly in the south.

Notes: Outside of the Cape Peninsula, where plants are generally small, this species grows up to 2 m.

Up to 50 cm   Aug–Jan

Cape Cowslip

Vierkleurtjie

Lachenalia aloides

(Hyacinth family – Hyacinthaceae)

An attractive, multicoloured bulbous **perennial**.

Leaves: 1–2 green, spreading, lance- to **strap-shaped** leaves with spots on the upper surface.

Flower head: Up to 10 cylindrical multicoloured flowers – red and yellow with green tips – hang on long flower stalks.

Distribution: Occasional.

Habitat: In crevices in the southern granite and sandstone mountain slopes.

Up to 40 cm   May–Oct

Aug–Nov · Up to 75 cm

Foetid Cape Tulip
Appelkoostulp
Moraea ochroleuca
(Iris family – Iridaceae)

A lovely, erect, robust **perennial**, with a branched stem.
Leaves: One, sometimes 2, narrow, **strap-like**, channelled, **basal** leaves; bend over and trail on the ground.
Flower head: Handsome, yet foul-smelling, flower, with 6 rounded, yellow petals and a deep yellow or red throat.
Distribution: Common, especially after fires.
Habitat: Lower slopes.

Sep–Jan · Up to 2 m

Hiker's Horror
Aspalathus chenopoda
(Pea family – Fabaceae)

A large, sturdy, bushy and distinctive shrub.
Leaves: Hairy, divided into 3 sharply pointed leaflets.
Flower head: Bright yellow flowers at ends of branches, in rounded terminal clusters.
Distribution: Fairly common.
Habitat: Mainly lower mountain slopes.
Notes: Before opening, flower head clusters look like sharply pointed green golf balls.

Jun–Oct · Up to 25 cm

Common Sorrel
Geelsuring
Oxalis pes-caprae
(Oxalis family – Oxalidaceae)

A common roadside plant, with many flowers on a long stalk.
Leaves: **Basal**, divided into 3 heart-shaped leaflets, hairy underneath, notched at tip.
Flower head: 3–20 all-yellow flowers on a single stalk.
Distribution: Common.
Habitat: Widespread, lower slopes on sandy and clay soils.
Notes: Found in grassy places and lawns. Regarded as a weed.

Woolly Rosinbush
Wolharpuisbos
Euryops pectinatus
(Daisy family – Asteraceae)

An attractive, large, rounded, green-grey shrub.
Leaves: Greenish grey, densely woolly; comb-like, toothed like a fern.
Flower head: Solitary, daisy-like flowers with bright yellow petals with yellow to orange-yellow centres; borne on long, bare flower stalks. Many flowers may appear on a single bush. Sticky to touch, resinous.
Distribution: Fairly common.
Habitat: On rocks and exposed ledges.

Up to 1.5 m   Sep–Dec

Rough Ragwort
Senecio rigidus
(Daisy family – Asteraceae)

A tall, sturdy, densely leaved shrub with coarse, hairy stems and leaves.
Leaves: Heavy, dark green, sandpaper-like, oblong-shaped, toothed; white-grey and woolly underneath, with prominent veins. Edges turn down.
Flower head: Numerous small, yellow flowers, orange-centred, massed at the top of the plant, in loose clusters.
Distribution: Frequently found.
Habitat: Upper and lower slopes.

Up to 2 m   Nov–Jan

Silver Pea
Xiphotheca fruticosa
(Pea family – Fabaceae)

A beautiful shrub with bright yellow flowers, underpinned by silver-grey leaves.
Leaves: Silver-grey, hairy, broad, somewhat oval, pointed.
Flower head: Bright, beautiful, canary-yellow pea-like flowers appear above leaves at branch tips in tightly packed, rounded clusters.
Distribution: Fairly common.
Habitat: Found on dampish soils, often in the mist belt.
Notes: Flowers well after fire.

Up to 2 m   Apr–Sep

Common Rosinbush
Geelmargriet
Euryops abrotanifolius
(Daisy family – Asteraceae)

An erect, bouquet-shaped shrub with few mid-branches and bare stems towards the base.
Leaves: Short, ascending leaves, narrow, thread-like, somewhat coral-like in shape.
Flower head: Bright yellow, single daisy flower with yellow, spreading petals, at ends of long flower stalks. Large clusters may be seen.
Distribution: Frequently found, very common.
Habitat: Widespread – particularly on rocks and exposed ledges.

Jun–Dec	Up to 2 m

Common Bulbine
Rooistorm
Bulbine alooides
(Aloe family – Asphodelaceae)

A small **geophyte** with many flowers.
Leaves: Long, **basal**, channelled, lance-shaped, often with hairy edges.
Flower head: Small, star-like, 6-petalled yellow flowers, each petal having a thin stripe down the centre; **inflorescence** vertically arranged. Flowers bloom and mature from the bottom upwards; each lasts a day.
Distribution: Frequently found.
Habitat: Widespread, lower slopes, rocky areas.

Feb–Oct	Up to 50 cm

Cape Weed
Botterblom
Arctotheca calendula
(Daisy family – Asteraceae)

An attractive, tufted, **perennial** shrub commonly regarded as a weed.
Leaves: Basal, in pairs opposite each other, green with white undersides and sharply toothed edges.
Flower head: Pale yellow flower with darker yellow inner ring and black centre; single flower occurs on a long, near-leafless stem.
Distribution: Fairly common.
Habitat: Mainly lower slopes and side of roads or disturbed soil.

Aug–Nov	Up to 20 cm

Sea Babooncress
Bobbejaankool
Othonna arborescens
(Daisy family – Asteraceae)

An erect, **succulent** shrub.
Leaves: Large, thick, fleshy, broadly oval; found clustered around flowering stem, at the base.
Flower head: Daisy-like, with 5 widely separated yellow petals and darker yellow centre; flowers borne at top of tall, green flower stem, well above the **basal** leaves.
Distribution: Occasional.
Habitat: Coastal dunes or among rocks.

Up to 60 cm | Jun–Oct

Yellow Margriet
Geelmargriet
Ursinia paleacea
(Daisy family – Asteraceae)

An erect, branched shrub.
Leaves: **Basal,** narrow, deeply divided, appearing feathery.
Flower head: Yellow centre and yellow petals; pinkish brown to orange-red underneath, especially at petal tips. Single flower borne at top of long, almost leafless, flower stalk.
Distribution: Frequently found.
Habitat: Damp rocky slopes.

Up to 90 cm | Jul–Apr

Common Tickberry
Bietou
Chrysanthemoides monilifera
(Daisy family – Asteraceae)

A large, rounded, spreading, semi-**succulent** shrub.
Leaves: **Simple,** dark green, leathery, somewhat oval, with toothed edges.
Flower head: Bright yellow flowers, with yellow centres and yellow, square-tipped petals; appear in groups of up to 5, towards end of branches.
Distribution: Common.
Habitat: Mainly lower dry mountain slopes.
Notes: Unlike most daisies, bears fruit – purple berries that resemble bloated ticks, hence the common name. *Chrysanthemoides monilifera* and *Osteospermum monilifera* refer to the same flower.

Up to 1.5 m | Apr–Oct

Aug–Dec | Up to 60 cm

Sea Cineraria
Cineraria geifolia
(Daisy family – Asteraceae)

A sprawling ground creeper.
Leaves: Pelargonium-type – broad, deeply indented, with long leaf stalks.
Flower head: All-yellow, small, flat-topped, daisy-like flowers with 8 petals grow on short stems. Usually found in small clusters.
Distribution: Common.
Habitat: Bushy and sheltered areas.

Jan–Dec | Up to 1 m

Holly-leaved Kidneyseed
Nephrotheca ilicifolia
(Daisy family – Asteraceae)

A sprawling, compactly leaved, aromatic shrub.
Leaves: Rough, tough, dry, hairy, broad and pointed, with wavy, toothed edges that roll backwards towards the underside.
Flower head: Yellow daisy-like flower with overlapping petals and orange centre emerges, singly, just above uppermost leaves.
Distribution: Frequently found.
Habitat: Widespread, upper slopes, plateaux and summits, often in dampish areas.
Notes: When rubbed, the leaves are aromatic.

Aug–Sep | Up to 2 m

Sickleleaf Conebush
Blinkblaartolbos
Leucadendron xanthoconus
(Protea family – Proteaceae)

A bright yellow, bushy shrub. Separate male and female plants.
Leaves: Narrow, flat, sword-like, bending inwards towards tips. Yellow in spring, red in summer, silver in autumn and winter.
Flower head: Cones are yellow or red with a silver sheen; seeds stored until plant is killed by fire.
Distribution: Frequently found.
Habitat: Upper and lower slopes.
Notes: Most abundant protea on the Cape Peninsula.

Buttonhole Saffronbush
Basbos
Gnidia oppositifolia
(Daphne family – Thymelaeaceae)

A thin, slender, supple shrub, found erect or bending over.
Leaves: Small, oval, opposite, overlapping, pointed, usually tinged dark red at the tips.
Flower head: 4–6 tiny, pale yellow, tubular flowers, each with 4 petals that fold back at the mouth, appear at tips of each branch.
Distribution: Occasional.
Habitat: Wet places, especially near stream banks.

Up to 3 m	Aug–Mar

Greater Rush Iris
Biesiesriet
Bobartia indica
(Iris family – Iridaceae)

An evergreen **perennial** with an erect, unbranched flower stem.
Leaves: Long, tough, thin, flat, **basal**, longer than the flower stem and trailing.
Flower head: Yellow, star-shaped, forming a dense cluster among the spiky leaves, at top of round, robust stems.
Distribution: Fairly common.
Habitat: Upper and lower slopes, widespread on mountain.
Notes: Flowers especially after fires.

Up to 1.3 m	Oct–Mar

Sour Fig
Perdevy
Carpobrotus edulis
(Ice Plant family – Aizoaceae)

A **succulent perennial** with trailing stems, spreading at ground level.
Leaves: Grass-green, fleshy, densely packed, triangular in cross-section, upward curving.
Flower head: Large, single, bright yellow flower with double row of thin petals that fade to pink with age.
Distribution: Common.
Habitat: Upper and lower slopes in fairly open, sandy, sunny areas.
Notes: Often seen on road verges, as a stabiliser.

Up to 15 cm	Jun–Jan

Apr–Jan | Up to 30 cm

Cape Hibiscus
Wildestokroos
Hibiscus aethiopicus
(Hibiscus family – Malvaceae)

A small, pretty, low-growing shrublet, with stems lying on ground.
Leaves: Thick, oval-oblong, with serrated edges.
Flower head: Cream to canary-yellow flower, with 5 broad, overlapping petals and dark yellow centre; borne, singly, on a short stem.
Distribution: Fairly common.
Habitat: Upper and lower stony sandstone or clay slopes.

Oct–Feb | Up to 20 cm

Cape Bogbean
Villarsia manningiana
(Bogbean family – Menyanthaceae)

A compact, brightly coloured flower with unusual petals.
Leaves: Large, oval, on long leaf stalks.
Flower head: Yellow flower with 5 feathery-edged, fringed petals.
Distribution: Occasional, only on Table Mountain.
Habitat: Grows in damp areas, often in seepage areas or near streams.
Notes: A look-alike species, *V. goldblattiana*, is found in Silvermine.

Oct–Jul | Up to 90 cm

Yellow Rice Heath
Geelrysheide
Erica lutea
(Erica family – Ericaceae)

An upright shrub, with many ascending branches covered with tiny flowers.
Leaves: Tiny, linear-shaped, opposite, pressing against branches.
Flower head: Mass of small pale yellow, white or off-white flowers, with 4 turned-back petals; flowers cluster towards the end of branches.
Distribution: Frequent.
Habitat: Upper mountain slopes, especially sandy areas.
Notes: The *E. lutea* in Silvermine are white, except for a few pink-tinged ones on Constantiaberg.

Teddybear Doll's Rose
Pokkiesblom
Hermannia hyssopifolia
(Hibiscus family – Malvaceae)

A somewhat twiggy shrub with many long, slender stems.
Leaves: Higher: oval and pointed; lower: larger, more wedge-shaped, toothed, powdery, dry, crumbly and well-veined.
Flower head: Many creamy or pale yellow, bell-like flowers that hang from soft hairy stems; clustered towards tops of branches.
Distribution: Fairly common.
Habitat: Moist or sheltered areas and south-facing slopes.

Up to 2 m   Jul–Nov

Wagon Tree
Waboom
Protea nitida
(Protea family – Proteaceae)

A tall shrub or small, cork-barked tree.
Leaves: Wide, leathery, hairless, bluish grey-green, oblong.
Flower head: Creamy coloured, bowl-shaped, resembling a shaving brush.
Distribution: Fairly common.
Habitat: Lower sandstone slopes.
Notes: 'Waboom' is an Afrikaans word for 'wagon tree'. The wood was used for wheel rims and brake blocks for ox wagons.

Up to 5 m   May–Sep

Polecat Strawflower
Geelsewejaartjie
Helichrysum foetidum
(Daisy family – Asteraceae)

An erect, robust, unpleasant-smelling shrub.
Leaves: Oblong, pointed, hairy above; grey-woolly underneath.
Flower head: 4–6 large, flat, yellow to cream flowers with creamy white 'petals' (**bracts**), borne in a large, loosely packed, flat-topped cluster.
Distribution: Fairly common.
Habitat: Damp mountain slopes or marshy areas.

Up to 1 m   Oct–May

Sep–Jan | Up to 60 cm

Soldier-in-the-box
Geldbeursie
Albuca flaccida
(Hyacinth family – Hyacinthaceae)

An attractive plant with drooping, yellow flowers on a slender stem.
Leaves: Two or 3, **basal**, long, broad, light green, deeply grooved or channelled.
Flower head: Bell-like, lightly scented flowers with green petals edged in yellow; touch of white on inner petals.
Distribution: Frequently found.
Habitat: Lower stony and sandy mountain slopes.

Aug–Nov | Up to 35 cm

Common Bonnet Orchid
Oumakappie
Pterygodium catholicum
(Orchid family – Orchidaceae)

An erect, unusual-looking flower with short, slender stem.
Leaves: Broad, oblong-pointed, semi-twisting, with wavy edges; partially **sheathed** stem that becomes reddish and spot-marked with age.
Flower head: 3–5 pale lemon-yellow, pungently scented flowers, each with a prominent hood resembling a bonnet, hang slightly downwards from top of plant's stem. Flower goes reddish with age.
Distribution: Occasional.
Habitat: All slopes, often in flat, damp, rocky areas.
Notes: Especially noticeable after fires.

Dec–May | Up to 1 m

Tinderleaf
Tontelblaar
Hermas villosa
(Carrot family – Apiaceae)

A tall, erect, single or multi-stemmed shrub.
Leaves: Large, shiny, dark green, **basal**, toothed, with edges curled under, furry grey-white underneath. Carrot-scented.
Flower head: Tiny lime-yellow flowers, densely packed in a rounded cluster in a head; forms at the top of a tall, pink, leafless stem, towering above the leaves.
Distribution: Fairly common.
Habitat: Upper and lower slopes.

Green Satyr Orchid
Soet trewwa
Satyrium odorum
(Orchid family – Orchidaceae)

A robust, upright plant in dense **spikes**.
Leaves: Fleshy, rounded, **basal**, **sheathing** and enclosing stem.
Flower head: All-green plant with green-yellow carnation-scented flowers emerging from top of the flower **spike**.
Distribution: Common.
Habitat: Upper and lower slopes. Found in semi-sheltered, granitic rocky areas.

Up to 55 cm Sep–Oct

Blister Bush
Bergseldery
Notobubon galbanum
(Carrot family – Apiaceae)

A large, erect, robust shrub with big leaves and a ball-shaped flower head. **Can cause severe blisters.**
Leaves: Light green, shiny, stalkless, celery-like with deeply incised edges.
Flower head: Small greenish-yellow flowers grow on thin firm stalks; spread out to form a rounded ball.
Distribution: Frequently found.
Habitat: Widespread, especially in bushy, damp, sheltered areas, such as ravines.
Notes: The sap makes skin ultra light-sensitive, so keep affected areas out of the sun.

Up to 3 m Sep–Feb

Green Sugarbush
Groenhofiesuikerbos
Protea coronata
(Protea family – Proteaceae)

An erect shrub or small tree with a hairy main stem.
Leaves: Upward-curving, spear-shaped, green leaves that become purple-tinged near and around the flower head.
Flower head: Large, bright green and white, somewhat hidden by the surrounding leaves. The only bright green Protea with a white 'bearded' tip found on the mountain.
Distribution: Occasional.
Habitat: High-rainfall areas, lower slopes, eastern areas. Likes clay soils.

Up to 3 m Jun–Oct

Bladder Heath

Erica halicacaba
(Erica family – Ericaceae)

A well-branched shrub with a thick, gnarled woody trunk; the brittle branches press against and cling to rocks.
Leaves: Finely pointed needle-like leaves borne on densely leafy branches.
Flower head: 1–3 large flowers, greenish-yellow turning brown, each about 6 mm long, hang down singly from a slender short stem, somewhat like an inflated bladder.
Distribution: Not often seen, but found on Table Mountain and more often on Silvermine.
Habitat: Rock crevices and ledges.
Notes: Grows even higher than 1 m in very old specimens.

Sep–Dec   Up to 1 m

Awl Saffron Bush

Gnidia juniperifolia
(Daphne family – Thymelaeaceae)

An attractive, erect, well-branched, spreading shrublet with 4-angled stems.
Leaves: Narrow, lance-shaped, alternately opposite, hairless leaves are loosely spread up a brown stem.
Flower head: 1–4 variably-sized, bright yellow, tubular flowers grow at branch tips.
Distribution: Frequent.
Habitat: Lower mountain slopes.

Jan–Dec   Up to 50 cm

Heather-leaved Gorse

Aspalathus ericifolia
(Pea family – Fabaceae)

A tall, erect shrub with branches curving upwards, often densely branched. The young branches have a shaggy-hairy or woolly appearance.
Leaves: Leaves are divided into 3 segments and are usually hairless or sparsely hairy. The leaf edges can sometimes be densely hairy.
Flower head: Single flowers with bright yellow petals emerge on side shoots towards the upper end of branches.
Distribution: Fairly common.
Habitat: Lower sandy and stony mountain slopes.

Sep–Nov   Up to 60 cm

Yellow Disa
Geeldisa
Disa tenuifolia
(Orchid family – Orchidaceae)

A slender, **tuberous perennial**.
Leaves: Narrow and tufted at the base with broader, lance-shaped leaves sheathing the flowering stem.
Flower head: Bright yellow with a slightly hooded upright petal with narrow wing-like petals each side; the middle petal (sepal) looks flat and heart-shaped.
Distribution: Occasional.
Habitat: Mountain seeps and damp, peaty soils.
Notes: Occurs especially after fires. Pollinated by carder and leaf-cutting bees.

Up to 30 cm — Nov–Feb

Sticky Green Heath
Groentaaiheide
Erica urna-viridis
(Erica family – Ericaceae)

An erect, sparingly branched, straggly, all-green shrub with long bare branches with leafy ends and long, almost leafless flower stalks.
Leaves: Ridged, keel-like leaves in **whorls** of 3–4.
Flower head: 3–4 large, sticky, pale yellowish green egg-shaped flowers, dark green at the tips, grow at the terminal ends of branches.
Distribution: Common in localised communities.
Habitat: Silvermine, limited to the Muizenberg mountains above Kalk Bay.
Notes: Endemic to Silvermine.

Up to 1 m+ — Jan–Dec

Common Ground Sugarbush
Protea acaulos
(Protea family – Proteaceae)

A small, prostrate shrub at ground level that appears to have no stem.
Leaves: Erect, variable, large, mostly paddle-shaped, often with a grey-green bloom; the leaf edges and central vein are reddish.
Flower head: Large, cup-shaped, yellowish, yeasty-smelling blooms, tips covered in woolly hairs, with the surround pinkish-red at the cup edges. Globe-shaped in bud.
Distribution: Fairly common, less so on Table Mountain.
Habitat: Lower, dry stony slopes.
Notes: Height refers to leaves above ground, not the flower head.

Up to 20 cm — Jul–Nov

HC

Sep–Oct | **Up to 2.6 m**

Peninsula Conebush
Rotstolbos
Leucadendron strobilinum
(Protea family – Proteaceae)

A robust shrub with a single purple stem.
Leaves: Broad, elliptic, dark green, backward-curving at their tips.
Flower head: Female: yellowish in green cone; male: smaller, with yellow petals going red towards tip, in smaller, fluffy cone.
Distribution: Frequently found.
Habitat: Mainly upper, damp, south-facing slopes, among large rocks.
Notes: Endemic to Cape Peninsula.

SR

Aug–Oct | **Up to 90 cm**

Knowltonia
Katjiedrieblaar, Tandpynblare
Knowltonia vesicatoria
(Ranunculus family – Ranunculaceae)

An unusual, near all-green flower.
Leaves: Dark green, leathery, oval to heart-shaped leaflets with toothed edges, in threes.
Flower head: White to creamy green flowers emerge from a common point on the main stem. Resembles a windmill.
Distribution: Fairly common.
Habitat: All slopes, in bush-shady areas or woody ravines.
Notes: The flowers produce hairless green berries that ripen to black.

CM

Apr–Sep | **Up to 40 cm**

Medusa's Head
Vingerpol
Euphorbia caput-medusae
(Euphorbia family – Euphorbiaceae)

A **succulent**, ground-hugging shrublet that resembles a clump of thick, rounded, pointing fingers.
Leaves: Has a few deciduous leaves.
Flower head: Lumpy cushion-like mass up to a metre wide, with intertwined branches; tiny flowers at end of branches. Has milky latex, considered poisonous.
Distribution: Rare – found only in a few locations. A 'special' for anyone visiting Lion's Head.
Habitat: Lower slopes. Grows on rocks on the dry northwest slopes.

Cape Everlasting
Syncarpha speciosissima
(Daisy family – Asteraceae)

An erect, easily seen shrublet, with a long, bare stem.
Occurs in clumps.
Leaves: Light grey-green, oblong, and hairy, pressed
against the stem at the base.
Flower head: Single, creamy white, well-petalled, disc-
shaped flower, with brown (earlier yellow) centre, on
a long stalk. Surrounding 'petals' (**bracts**) are sharply
pointed.
Distribution: Common.
Habitat: Open areas among bushes, on upper slopes.
Notes: An 'everlasting' flower when cut.

Up to 60 cm   Jul–Jan

Black-bearded Sugarbush
Swartbaardsuikerbos
Protea lepidocarpodendron
(Protea family – Proteaceae)

An upright, single-stemmed, well-branched shrub or
small tree.
Leaves: Long, narrow, grey-green, upward-pointing,
somewhat sword-shaped.
Flower head: Handsome bearded protea, purple-
black and white head sticking out of leaves at top
of sturdy stem.
Distribution: Fairly common.
Habitat: Upper and lower slopes in **kloofs**, sheltered and
moist areas.

Up to 2 m   Apr–Dec

Wild Cotton
Katoenbos
Gomphocarpus cancellatus
(Milkweed family – Apocynaceae)

A large, erect, leafy, stiff-looking, hairy shrub.
Leaves: Green-grey, broad, oblong, leathery, well-veined,
in pairs opposite, alternately overlapping those below,
whitish underside.
Flower head: Unusual-looking cream and brown flowers
occur in a hanging cluster at top of plant. Flowers have
5 small tubes. Bears purple fruit.
Distribution: Occasional.
Habitat: Lower rocky slopes.
Notes: Has milky sap and thorny, fig-shaped seed pod.

Up to 1.5 m   Mar–Oct

CM

May–Jul — Up to 45 cm

Brown Afrikaner
Bruinafrikaner
Gladiolus maculatus
(Iris family – Iridaceae)

A slender **perennial**, generally flowering in winter.
Leaves: Three or 4 narrow, leathery, short-bladed leaves, 2 **basal**, the lowermost sheathing the lower half of the stem. Leafless at flowering time.
Flower head: Strongly scented, long-tubed, funnel-shaped, brownish-yellow, with many brown or purple-brown spots. This colouring of the flowers can be very variable, and occasionally the brown pigment is missing, leaving yellow flowers.
Distribution: Frequent in localised areas, especially in the south.
Habitat: Lower mountain slopes.
Notes: Pollinated by moths.

CM

May–Dec — Up to 50 cm

Cat's Tail Bush
Katstert
Microdon dubius
(Sutera family – Scrophulariaceae)

A soft, wand-like, branched **perennial** with stems that are minutely hairy.
Leaves: Small, thin, narrow, lance-shaped – borne on a reddish-brown, notched woody stem.
Flower head: Tiny, curved, fragrant, 5-lobed, tubular-shaped flowers, yellow in colour but often with maroon to brownish petals, are borne on an elongated **spike**. The flowers give off distinctive sweet scent at night.
Distribution: Common.
Habitat: On sandstone slopes.

CM

Dec–Mar — Up to 1 m

Rock Phylica
Hardebos
Phylica dioica
(Phylica family – Ramnaceae)

A rigid, much-branched shrub, branches buff-hairy.
Leaves: Dense, long, fairly large and broad, egg-shaped, rough-hairy above, white-woolly below, leaf edges slightly turned down.
Flower head: Many small, white flowers are borne at the end of branches and surrounded by leaves.
Distribution: Occasional.
Habitat: In rocky places on upper mountain slopes.

Rough Chincherichee

Growwetjienk

Ornithogalum hispidum
(Hyacinth family – Hyacinthaceae)

An attractive, sparsely-leaved bulbous **geophyte** with a long stalk.
Leaves: 2–4 oval-shaped leaves at the base of the plant sheathe each other; those higher up, lance-shaped, wither at the time of flowering.
Flower head: White flowers, 6-petalled, with a dull greenish stripe outside that fades to brown. Grows on long flower stalks, collectively forming a loose **inflorescence** of 2–20 flowers at the terminal end.
Distribution: Common.
Habitat: Lower slopes and clay or low rocky outcrops.
Notes: Flowers especially after fires.

Up to 45 cm | Nov–Feb

Dark-eyed Ixia

Ixia polystachya
(Iris family – Iridaceae)

A tall, slender **geophyte** with 1–4 branched stems carrying a spike of flowers of variable colouration.
Leaves: Variable in size and shape, often long and narrow, lance- to sword-shaped.
Flower head: One-to-many, faintly scented, 6-petalled flowers, usually white, but also in shades of pink, mauve, or purple, are borne at the top of a lax **spike**. The flower centres can be green, blue, purple, pink, yellow or white.
Distribution: Frequent on Table Mountain, less common in the south; favours eastern slopes.
Habitat: Damp or shady areas on sandstone or granite soils on the mountain and flats.

Up to 80 cm | Oct–Dec

Flat-topped Bitterbush

Selago corymbosa
(Sutera family – Scrophulariaceae)

An erect, densely-leaved, sturdy shrublet with minutely hairy stems.
Leaves: Leaves in tufts, needle-like, spreading, somewhat bottlebrush-looking from a distance.
Flower head: Many tiny white flowers with yellow **stamens** cluster on several branchlets to form a dense, flat-topped to rounded **inflorescence**.
Distribution: Fairly common.
Habitat: Stony flats and slopes.

Up to 60 cm | Dec–May

Silver Tree
Witteboom
Leucadendron argenteum
(Protea family – Proteaceae)

A handsome tree with a stout trunk, thick, grey-coloured bark and silvery-looking leaves. Separate male and female plants.
Leaves: Soft, shiny, green-grey, long, tapering, covered with fine silvery hairs.
Flower head: Female identified by a large, silver, egg-shaped cone surrounded by long leaves; male (shown here) is considerably smaller and less obvious.
Distribution: Occasional.
Habitat: Lower sunny slopes, mainly forest margins; damp, granite and clay soils.
Notes: Endangered. Endemic to the Peninsula.

| Sep–Oct | Up to 10 m |

Marsh Bulbinella
Katstert
Bulbinella nutans
(Aloe family – Asphodelaceae)

A tall, **perennial** herb.
Leaves: Bright green, long, **strap-like**, channelled.
Flower head: Mass of white and yellow (rarely orange), unscented flowers, in an elongated head, at end of long, green, leafless flower stem. Often found in clumps. Flowers are short lived.
Distribution: Fairly common on Table Mountain.
Habitat: Occurs in moist areas such as stream banks, seeps and soggy soils.

| Sep–Oct | Up to 1 m |

Green Violet
Groenviooltjie
Lachenalia fistulosa
(Hyacinth family – Hyacinthaceae)

A bulbous **geophyte**.
Leaves: Two, broad, sometimes brown-spotted, like an extended spotted tongue.
Flower head: Bell-like, cream, blue, yellow or violet scented flowers, with brown markings.
Distribution: Fairly common.
Habitat: Mainly lower western slopes in clay soils.

| Sep–Oct | Up to 30 cm |

Fragrant Crassula
Klipblom
Crassula fascicularis
(Crassula family – Crassulaceae)

A small, erect, **perennial succulent**.
Leaves: Small, lance-shaped, semi-**succulent**, hairy-edged, ascending the red stem.
Flower head: Jasmine-like flowers, white, cream, or pinkish, loosely clustered together in a rounded to flat-topped, multi-flowered **inflorescence**, like a bouquet, at end of flower stem. Scented in evening.
Distribution: Fairly common.
Habitat: Mainly lower slopes, especially sandstone.
Notes: Buds appear dull red.

| Up to 40 cm | Sep–Dec |

Anaxeton

Anaxeton laeve
(Daisy family – Asteraceae)

A small, woolly shrublet with a long flower stalk.
Leaves: Thin, stalkless, upward curving, grey-green, with shiny upper surfaces and woolly underneath.
Flower head: Small, red-backed flowers in bud, densely packed in a tight, round-headed cluster, turning white when open.
Distribution: Frequently found.
Habitat: Widespread, mainly upper slopes, but also plateaux and summits.

| Up to 45 cm | Apr–Oct |

White Bristle Bush
Blombos
Metalasia muricata
(Daisy family – Asteraceae)

A common, erect, rigid, thin-stemmed, multi-branched, densely leaved shrub.
Leaves: Green-grey, lance-shaped, hook-tipped, curving upwards.
Flower head: Dull white, woolly, brown underneath, in somewhat rounded clusters at top of branches. Honey-scented.
Distribution: Frequently found.
Habitat: Widespread, upper and lower slopes.

| Up to 2 m | Apr–Sep |

CM

Aug–Oct | Up to 50 cm

China Flower
Bergskaapboegoe
Adenandra uniflora
(Citrus family – Rutaceae)

An evergreen, sparsely branched, aromatic shrublet.
Leaves: Small, soft, oval, with rolled-down edges. Spot markings on leaves.
Flower head: Single flower, glistening white, 5 rounded petals with red centre and veins. Undersides pink. Red buds.
Distribution: Frequently found.
Habitat: Mainly lower slopes, in northwestern drier areas.
Notes: Lookalike, *A. villosa*, is taller, bears clusters of flowers; flat leaves, often hairy on underside.

GN

Aug–Dec | Up to 60 cm

Painted Lady
Bergpypie
Gladiolus carneus
(Iris family – Iridaceae)

An erect, **perennial** herb. The best-known gladiolus on the mountain.
Leaves: Long, thin, partially **sheathing** the stem. Single **basal** leaf appears after flowering.
Flower head: Pink or white touched with pink, with a pale pink, funnel-shaped throat. Lower petals have variable red markings, on the inside, like an inverted wine glass.
Distribution: Fairly common.
Habitat: Upper slopes, mainly eastern side, sheltered areas.
Notes: Especially noticeable after fires.

HC

Oct–Apr | Up to 30 cm

The Mexican
Erigeron karvinskianus
(Daisy family – Asteraceae)

A pretty, non-indigenous daisy.
Leaves: Light green, narrowly oval, pointed, alternate.
Flower head: Daisy-like, with a white, sometimes purple, ring of petals and yellow centre. Grows singly or in small clumps.
Distribution: Occasional.
Habitat: Mainly southeastern areas along service roads and footpaths.
Notes: An immigrant from Mexico, hence its coined name.

Cape Snowdrop
Skaamblommetjie
Crassula capensis
(Crassula family – Crassulaceae)

A small, delicate, erect, **tuberous perennial**.
Leaves: Relatively large, green with purple underneath, rounded, ground-hugging, with a scalloped edge.
Flower head: Small, snowy white, cup-shaped, 6-petalled flowers on red flower stalks; form in a loose cluster at the top of a **spike**. Some flowers bend over and droop.
Distribution: Occasional.
Habitat: Occurs in sheltered damp areas.

| Up to 15 cm | Jun–Aug |

Cape Anemone
Syblom
Anemone tenuifolia
(Ranunculus family – Ranunculaceae)

A sturdy, tufted **perennial** with feathery petals.
Leaves: **Basal**, dark green, toothed, divided into many segments.
Flower head: Pinkish white silky petals and bright yellow to brown centre; petal undersides are darker pink. Single flower borne on a long, pinkish velvety stem.
Distribution: Fairly common.
Habitat: Upper slopes, mainly on eastern side in good rainfall areas.

| Up to 60 cm | Jun–Nov |

Larkspur Baroe
Fraaibaroe
Cyphia bulbosa
(Bellflower family – Campanulaceae)

A small, delicate, mauve-white **perennial**.
Leaves: Few, at base, deeply incised, and well-spaced, getting smaller up the stem.
Flower head: Small, funnel-shaped flowers, with flared 2-lipped mouth; occur alternately up the stem.
Distribution: Fairly common.
Habitat: Upper and lower slopes. Bushy, damp and sheltered areas.
Notes: Occurs often after fire.

| Up to 40 cm | Aug–Oct |

CM

Wild Buchu
Rooiboegoe
Diosma hirsuta
(Citrus family – Rutaceae)

A small, erect, bushy, aromatic shrublet.
Leaves: Small, narrow, *alternate* leaves tipped with a short, sharp point.
Flower head: Numerous tiny, white cup-like flowers, with pink-red flower stalks, occur scattered towards the ends of branchlets.
Distribution: Fairly common.
Habitat: Clay and sandstone slopes.
Notes: *D. oppositifolia* is similar – a bigger plant with short leaves in neat rows, each pair *alternately opposite*. Flowers, mainly in pairs, with green centre.

| Apr–Sep | Up to 50 cm |

HC

False Slugwort
Basterslakblom
Dischisma ciliatum
(Sutera family – Scrophulariaceae)

An erect annual or **perennial** with a mass of feathery white flowers.
Leaves: Narrow, spreading, alternate.
Flower head: Numerous small, white flowers emerge from the sides of a tall green flower **spike**, surrounding its upper half with a frilly whiteness.
Distribution: Fairly common.
Habitat: Upper and lower slopes.
Notes: *Hebenstreita cordata* is a lookalike; has red spot-marks on the white flowers.

| Aug–Dec | Up to 40 cm |

GN

Little Sundew
Kleinsnotrosie
Drosera trinervia
(Sundew family – Droseraceae)

An **insectivorous** herb.
Leaves: **Basal**, covered with glandular hairs that secrete sticky fluid; attract and trap small insects that are absorbed by the plant.
Flower head: 2–10 small white flowers, each with 5 broad, rounded petals.
Distribution: Common.
Habitat: Mostly upper slopes, in damp, wind-sheltered areas.

| Sep–Dec | Up to 10 cm |

Common Button Daisy
Ganskos
Cotula turbinata
(Daisy family – Asteraceae)

A tiny, unmistakable annual.
Leaves: Thin, fine, **pinnate** or forked, thread-like, emerging on alternate sides of stem.
Flower head: Single, yellow-centred flower with tiny white or yellow petals, on slender flower stalk. Often found in clumps.
Distribution: Common.
Habitat: Widespread, mainly lower slopes, sunny areas.
Notes: Often regarded as a weed.

| Up to 30 cm | Jul–Nov |

Cape Geranium
Vrouebossie
Geranium incanum
(Geranium family – Geraniaceae)

A widely spreading, evergreen **perennial**, a ground cover, with multi-branched stems.
Leaves: Thin, much divided, green above, grey below, on long leaf stalks.
Flower head: White, 5 broad petals with marked veins; usually solitary, appear on thin stalks above leaves. Petals have a notch, or dent, at their tips.
Distribution: Rare – found only in a few locations.
Habitat: Sandy and stony soils.
Notes: Flowers can be purple or pink, variable in size.

| Up to 30 cm | Aug–Nov |

Helichrysum
Helichrysum fruticans
(Daisy family – Asteraceae)

An erect, woolly shrub with multiple flower heads.
Leaves: Broad, oval, grey-green, woolly.
Flower head: White flowers with yellow centres, crowded together in a large, tightly bunched head, at end of an almost naked flower stem.
Distribution: Frequently found.
Habitat: Upper and lower slopes.

| Up to 50 cm | Sep–Feb |

Pelargonium
Fynblaarmalva
Pelargonium myrrhifolium var. *myrrhifolium*
(Geranium family – Geraniaceae)

A low-growing **perennial** with hairy flower stalks.
Leaves: Variable in size, deeply **lobed** or fragmented.
Flower head: Up to 6 white flowers, with 2 large upper petals streaked with red veins; well above the leaves.
Distribution: Frequently found.
Habitat: Often found sheltering under bushes or near stony sand footpaths.
Notes: Var. *coriandrifolium* is similar but with pinkish purple flowers and red-edged leaves.

Jan–Dec	Up to 30 cm

White Romulea
Witknikkertjie
Romulea flava
(Iris family – Iridaceae)

An erect, **perennial** herb.
Leaves: Thread-like, with narrow grooves; taller than the flower.
Flower head: White, with 6 petals, yellow cup (throat), on single flower stem.
Distribution: Occasional.
Habitat: Lower slopes, common in grassy areas.
Notes: Yellow form also found but not common.

Jun–Oct	Up to 30 cm

Drumsticks
Verfblommetjie
Zaluzianskya capensis
(Sutera family – Scrophulariaceae)

A short-lived annual whose flowers, resembling kettledrum sticks, remain closed during the day and open at night.
Leaves: Tiny, narrow, irregularly edged, stalkless.
Flower head: White inside, dark red outside, with 5 deeply notched petals; open at dusk and emit a strong scent.
Distribution: Fairly common.
Habitat: Often found in shady areas among bushes.
Notes: Pollinated by moths.

Jun–Nov	Up to 40 cm

Arctotis
Taaigousblom
Arctotis aspera
(Daisy family – Asteraceae)

A sprawling shrub with a leafy stem.
Leaves: Irregularly shaped, deeply **lobed**, hairy, covered with bristles.
Flower head: Single daisy flower with white petals (red to purple underside) and yellow centre, on a green flower stalk.
Distribution: Fairly common.
Habitat: Mountain slopes; widespread, especially in the drier northern areas.

| Up to 1 m | Aug–Oct |

Twining Baroe
Bergbaroe
Cyphia volubilis
(Bellflower family – Campanulaceae)

A small, climbing **perennial** herb.
Leaves: Slender, hairless, **simple**, lance-shaped, growing from the stem in sets of 3.
Flower head: Series of single white flowers, with dark blue **stamens**, on short stems; spaced along the twining shoot. Flowers can also be blue, purple, pink.
Distribution: Fairly common.
Habitat: Lower slopes, bushy areas.

| Up to 60 cm | Aug–Oct |

Wild Rosemary
Kapokbossie
Eriocephalus africanus
(Daisy family – Asteraceae)

An evergreen, multi-branched, twiggy shrub.
Leaves: Small, narrow, silvery green, hairy, aromatic, in tufts along the branches.
Flower head: Small white flowers, with roughly scalloped petals and reddish brown centres; form in small clusters at branch tips. Flower head is fluffy or woolly at fruiting time.
Distribution: Fairly common.
Habitat: Lower, dry western, granitic slopes.
Notes: Birds use the fluffy seed heads for nest lining.

| Up to 1 m | Apr–Oct |

CW

Sep–Oct | Up to 50 cm

Star-eyed Aristea

Aristea spiralis
(Iris family – Iridaceae)

An attractive, erect **perennial** with large flowers.
Leaves: Spear-shaped, fairly wide and soft, **sheathing** the flowering stem.
Flower head: White (or pale blue) flower has 6 big oval petals with purple markings and orange **anthers**.
Distribution: Fairly common.
Habitat: Upper and lower slopes, often found in clumps.
Notes: Flowers open in the morning, then twist into a spiral as they fade.

HC

May–Dec | Up to 1 m

Pine-leaved Saffronbush

Gnidia pinifolia
(Daphne family – Thymelaeaceae)

An erect, leafy, single-stemmed shrub.
Leaves: Short, thin, pine-like, crowded, alternately opposite each other, gradually tapering to a sharp tip.
Flower head: Ten or more small, white, tubular flowers, each with 4 petals, clustered in a terminal head at the branch tips. Immature flowers can be pinkish in bud.
Distribution: Fairly common.
Habitat: Upper and lower slopes.

HC

Jan–Dec | Up to 1 m

Mountain Saffronbush

Gnidia tomentosa
(Daphne family – Thymelaeaceae)

A tall, erect, leafy, branching shrub with a reddish brown stem.
Leaves: Soft, narrowly oval, pointed, alternate, overlapping, rising up the flowering stem.
Flower head: White, trumpet-shaped flower, with 4 small, bright yellow 'petals' standing upright in the centre, flaring at the end in 4 parts.
Distribution: Fairly common.
Habitat: Upper and lower slopes, often near streams or in damp areas.

Moraea
Rietuintjie
Moraea tricuspidata
(Iris family – Iridaceae)

A lovely, **cormous geophyte** on an erect slender stem.
Leaves: Single, **basal**, thin, channelled, hairless.
Flower head: Distinct white to cream unscented flower, with 3 broad petals, brown-speckled at the centre; borne at the top of a firm, slender stem.
Distribution: Fairly common; occasional in Silvermine.
Habitat: Lower slopes.
Notes: Flowers especially after fires.

| Up to 60 cm | Sep–Oct |

Mountain Lazybush
Sukkelbossie
Oftia africana
(Sutera family – Scrophulariaceae)

A sprawling shrub with trailing branches often spreading over, or between, large rocks.
Leaves: Stiff, stalkless, narrowly oval, with sharply toothed edges.
Flower head: Nondescript white flower with 5 petals and pale green throat; borne, singly, at tips of branches. Chocolate-scented fragrance.
Distribution: Common.
Habitat: Lower slopes on rocky sandstone and granite.

| Up to 1 m | Jan–Dec |

Chincherinchee
Tjienk
Ornithogalum thyrsoides
(Hyacinth family – Hyacinthaceae)

A popular, commercially sold, bulbous **perennial**.
Leaves: Basal, broad, lance-shaped and often leaning outwards; have slightly hairy edges. Sometimes dry at time of flowering.
Flower head: Large, creamy white, bowl-shaped flowers with 6 oval-pointed petals, often with green-brown centres that fade with age; grow together in tightly bunched clusters, at the top of flower stems.
Distribution: Fairly common.
Habitat: Damp, partly shady, sandy places on lower slopes.

| Up to 80 cm | Oct–Dec |

Jun–Oct | Up to 1 m

Wild Aster
Wilde-aster
Polyarrhena reflexa
(Daisy family – Asteraceae)

A straggling shrub.
Leaves: Small, oblong to lance-shaped, slightly hairy, bending backwards. Leaf edges are scratchy.
Flower head: Small daisy flower with white petals, purple-red on reverse, and yellow centre; forms at the end of short stem.
Distribution: Fairly common.
Habitat: Lower slopes, especially in damp areas.

Jul–Dec | From 40–80 cm

Wild Tobacco
Wildetabak
Silene undulata
(Carnation family – Caryophyllaceae)

An erect, rather sticky, sprawling **perennial** with distinctly notched petals.
Leaves: Long, thin, hairy, lance-shaped, alternately opposite, spaced up the stem.
Flower head: White (or pink/red) 5-petalled flower, each petal deeply **lobed** so it looks V-shaped.
Distribution: Common.
Habitat: In shady places and on slopes.
Note: This flower has a short and long form, hence the height range.

Sep–Dec | Up to 60 cm

Common Starheath
Altydbos
Staavia radiata
(Brunia family – Bruniaceae)

An erect shrublet with a leafy stem and short thin branchlets.
Leaves: Small, narrow, lance-shaped, brown-tipped, pointing upwards.
Flower head: Tiny, white, daisy-like flower with dark red-purple centre. Often found in clumps.
Distribution: Occasional.
Habitat: Widespread, often found on sandy soils and dampish areas.

100

Calycina

Erica calycina
(Erica family – Ericaceae)

An erect shrublet with many semi-erect, rigid branches.
Leaves: Small, linear-shaped, ascending, tightly packed, in groups of 3.
Flower head: Showy, plentiful, white, bell-shaped flowers with dusky 'mouths' (caused by dark **anthers**), in groups of 3, at end of small branches.
Distribution: Frequently found.
Habitat: Upper slopes and summits, rocky areas.

| Up to 2 m | Jul–Dec |

Cape Snow
Witsewejaartjie
Syncarpha vestita
(Daisy family – Asteraceae)

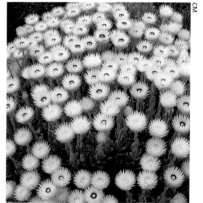

A compact, multi-branched, densely leafed shrub.
Leaves: Ascending, woolly grey-green, long, **strap-like**, overlapping, dark-tipped.
Flower head: Large, rounded, 'everlasting' flower with papery, white, pointed 'petals' (**bracts**) and purple-red centre that goes brown with age. Flower is borne on a sturdy, grey, woolly stem.
Distribution: Fairly common.
Habitat: Upper slopes.
Notes: The flowers, when cut, last more or less for ever.

| Up to 1 m | Oct–Jan |

Common Buttonbush
Vleiknoppiesbos
Berzelia lanuginosa
(Brunia family – Bruniaceae)

A large, evergreen, densely leaved, multi-branched shrub.
Leaves: Tiny, thin, black-tipped, upward curving; press against soft flexible branches.
Flower head: Tiny, creamy white, fluffy, ball-shaped flowers grow profusely in tight clusters at branch tips and go brown with age.
Distribution: Frequently found.
Habitat: Damp slopes, stream banks, and near water.
Notes: Similar to *Brunia noduliflora* but flower heads smaller, leaves softer when brushed.

| Up to 2 m | Jun–Dec |

Stompie
Brunia noduliflora
(Brunia family – Bruniaceae)

An erect, spreading shrublet with moderately hairy branches and ball-shaped flowers.
Leaves: Tiny, small, black-tipped, hard-textured, pointed, tightly packed among the stiff branches.
Flower head: Creamy white, fluffy balls when young; turn brown around August as the flower dies, then grey-black. Fragrant.
Distribution: Occasional.
Habitat: Rocky mountain slopes.
Notes: Differs from lookalike *Berzelia lanuginosa,* being smaller, more robust, with bigger flowers. Not associated with water.

Jun–Oct	Up to 1.5 m

Confetti Bush
Klipboegoe
Coleonema album
(Citrus family – Rutaceae)

A large, erect, multi-branched, rounded, bushy shrub.
Leaves: Small, alternate, narrow and copious. The gland-dotted leaves rise up the reddish branch stems.
Flower head: Mass of small, white, sweet-scented flowers with dark green centres, spread – like thrown confetti – over the bush at branch tips. Petals veined with pink; buds pinkish.
Distribution: Common.
Habitat: Found especially among granite outcrops and rocky ledges.

Jun–Dec	Up to 1.8 m

Snow Daisy
Wildewitmargriet
Dimorphotheca nudicaulis
(Daisy family – Asteraceae)

A large, **perennial** daisy.
Leaves: Long, somewhat ragged, lance-shaped, with toothed edges; crowd the base of the flower.
Flower head: Single flowers with gleaming white petals and orange to purple-black centres, on a long, bare flower stalk. Petal undersides are purple to copper-coloured.
Distribution: Fairly common.
Habitat: Sunny open areas.
Notes: *D. pluvialis* is very similar but petal underside is darker and more purple.

Aug–Nov	Up to 30 cm

Wild Clove Bush
Bergklappers
Montinia caryophyllacea
(Montinia family – Montinaceae)

An erect, thin shrublet.
Leaves: Blue-green, longish, oblong pointed, alternate, with well-defined mid-vein.
Flower head: Somewhat sparse, small, white, 4-petalled flowers at tips of branches.
Distribution: Common.
Habitat: Mainly lower mountain slopes.

Up to 1.5 m | Jun–Dec

Marsh Daisy
Belskruie
Osmitopsis asteriscoides
(Daisy family – Asteraceae)

A tall, sturdy, upright, loosely branched, camphor-scented shrub.
Leaves: Lower stem leafless; upper stems well-branched with crowded, oval-pointed, hairy leaves.
Flower head: Daisy-like flowers, with white petals and a yellow centre, borne towards top of plant on short side branches.
Distribution: Common.
Habitat: Found in dense stands near streams, seeps and in marshy areas.

Up to 2 m | Aug–Dec

Featherhead
Veerkoppie
Phylica pubescens
(Phylica family – Rhamnaceae)

An attractive shrub, densely covered with soft, feathery, unmatted hairs.
Leaves: Grey-green, narrow, hairy, pointed; edges turn downwards.
Flower head: Pale to creamy yellow, fluffy flowers in a solitary flower head; resembles a small feather duster.
Distribution: Occasional.
Habitat: Mainly lower eastern slopes.

Up to 2 m | Apr–Dec

Jul–Nov | Up to 1.2 m

Grey Stilbe
Stilbe vestita
(Stilbe family – Stilbaceae)

An erect shrub with upright branches and a 'bottlebrush' flower head.
Leaves: Densely crowded, overlapping, needle-like leaves.
Flower head: Erect, oval **spike** with fluffy, creamy white flowers crowded towards top. After flowering, top end of the flower stem remains vertical – resembles a candlestick.
Distribution: Occasional.
Habitat: Damp sandstone slopes.

Jan–Dec | Up to 1.5 m

Whip-stemmed Featherhead
Katstertjie
Struthiola ciliata
(Daphne family – Thymelaeaceae)

A tall, thin shrublet.
Leaves: Closely packed, small, lance-shaped, sometimes reddish at their tips; press against and **sheathe** entire erect stem.
Flower head: Many small, creamy white (or pink), tubular flowers with 4 squarish petals; flowers emerge, and bend out, from upper sides to top of flower **spike**. Evening-scented.
Distribution: Frequently found.
Habitat: Widespread, upper and lower slopes.

Jun–Dec | Up to 1.2 m

Arum Lily
Varkblom
Zantedeschia aethiopica
(Arum family – Araceae)

A handsome, well-known white flower.
Leaves: Dark green, broadly arrowhead-shaped, on long, spongy leaf stalks.
Flower head: Single, large, white petal surrounds a small central yellow column. Often found in clumps.
Distribution: Fairly common.
Habitat: Seasonally damp, shady, sheltered areas, among rocks and bushes.
Notes: Wild porcupines eat the bulb.

Common Paperflower
Sewejaartjie
Edmondia sesamoides
(Daisy family – Asteraceae)

An erect, lightly-branched shrublet with a grey-white stem.
Leaves: Basal, narrow, lying open, leaf edges curling up; higher: small, overlapping, pressing against flower stem.
Flower head: Central part white (or yellow), surrounded by layers of silky white (or pink), reflective, papery petals. Pink in bud.
Distribution: Common.
Habitat: Open sunny areas.

| Up to 40 cm | Aug–Jan |

Black-eyed Susan
Terblanzbossie
Hibiscus trionum
(Hibiscus family – Malvaceae)

An attractive annual found very low down the mountain.
Leaves: Deeply cut, **compound** leaves, in 3 leaflets, varying in size.
Flower head: Creamy flower, with 5 veined petals and a dark centre; grows on a firm, hairy stem.
Distribution: Rare, on lower slopes.
Habitat: Forest margins and damp places.
Notes: Not indigenous to the Cape.

| Up to 50 cm | Sep–Dec |

Common Sunshine Conebush
Geelbos
Leucadendron salignum
(Protea family – Proteaceae)

A small, variable, multi-stemmed plant, often only about 0.5 m high.
Leaves: Long, smooth, narrow, pointed, alternate, twisting. During flowering, upper leaves turn ivory, yellow or red.
Flower head: Distinguished from other multi-stemmed Sunshine Conebushes by its silver-grey cones, and the conspicuous cup around the cones.
Distribution: Fairly common.
Habitat: Upper and lower slopes, in open sunny areas.
Notes: The most widespread *Leucadendron* in South Africa.

| Up to 2 m | Apr–Nov |

Jan–Jun | Up to 90 cm

Wild Asparagus
Wag-'n-bietjie
Asparagus rubicundus
(Asparagus family – Asparagaceae)

A tall, erect, spiny shrub with smooth, glossy, dark reddish-brown, hairless stems that are covered with spreading spines.
Leaves: Minute, curved, spine-like leaves are borne on the woody stem and branches.
Flower head: Tiny, white, fragrant, long-stalked flowers with 6 drooping petals are widely dispersed about the shrub. The flowers give rise to red berries.
Distribution: Common.
Habitat: Grows on sandy and granite lower slopes, especially to the south and occasionally in wooded areas.

Jan–Dec | Up to 50cm

Skunk Bush
Stinkbossie
Chaenostoma hispidum
(Sutera family – Scrophulariaceae)

A small shrublet with many erect or sprawling branches.
Leaves: Roughly toothed, oval to elliptically shaped; grow in pairs opposite each other.
Flower head: White to pink/mauve flowers with a yellow funnel-shaped throat.
Distribution: Common.
Habitat: Common among bushes on sandy slopes.

Aug–Oct | Up to 50 cm

Little Painted Lady
Vlinderpypie
Gladiolus debilis
(Iris family – Iridaceae)

An attractive, slender **perennial** with zigzagging stems.
Leaves: 1–2 lower leaves that can reach almost as high as the stems, and 2 higher leaves, shorter, narrower and thicker.
Flower head: 1–3 unscented, white (occasionally pink), long-tubed flowers grow together, each having red arrowhead or spade-like markings on their lower petals (tepals).
Distribution: Frequent in specific localities.
Habitat: Rocky sandstone slopes on Silvermine plateau.

Ker-ker

Erica imbricata
(Erica family – Ericaceae)

A distinctive, erect, robust shrub with prolific flower-bearing branches.
Leaves: Short, in **whorls** of 3 facing upwards.
Flower head: Flowers, usually white, with distinctive dark brown **anthers** characteristically protruding. Flowers cluster in threes (or more) on small, densely leafy, lateral branches and at the ends of upper branchlets.
Distribution: Frequent. Widespread.
Habitat: Fairly dry, sandy conditions on hills and mountain slopes.
Notes: Known as ker-ker because of the sound made when brushing up against the plants.

Up to 50 cm — Feb–Oct

Box Heath

Erica pyxidiflora
(Erica family – Ericaceae)

An erect shrublet with a cylindrical head; upright, hairless branches and copious leaves.
Leaves: Short, thick, hairy, inward curving; ascending in sixes that densely crowd the topmost branches from which flowers emerge.
Flower head: Stalkless, pale pink to white urn-shaped flowers with a wide, rounded mouth showing dark **anthers**; emerge through the leaves of long, erect branches.
Distribution: Occasional
Habitat: Found in damp, soggy or marshy conditions and near streams on Table Mountain and Silvermine, such as on the Steenberg plateau.

Up to 60 cm — May–Dec

Bladder Cell Stonecrop

Crassula pruinosa
(Crassula family – Crassulaceae)

A slightly woody **perennial** with hairy backward-bending branches when young; wiry stems and attractive flowers.
Leaves: Dull green, stalkless, widely spaced, alternately opposite, somewhat lance-shaped leaves grow up a brown stem.
Flower head: Many white tubular flowers in a flat-topped cluster with prominent red **stamens**; yellow when still opening.
Distribution: Occasional.
Habitat: Rocky areas on the lower slopes.

Up to 30 cm — Oct–Feb

Feb–Apr | Up to 30 cm

Grey Pin Buchu
Macrostylis villosa
(Citrus family – Rutaceae)

An attactive, compact aromatic shrub with long-lasting white flower clusters.
Leaves: Ascending, overlapping, lance-shaped, short-stalked, hairy or hairless, gland-dotted.
Flower head: White or cream flowers in terminal clusters of 11–18 at branch tips with a beard-like tuft of hairs near the middle of the petals; **stamens** protrude beyond the flowers increasingly with age.
Distribution: Frequent.
Habitat: Stony mountain areas.

Nov–Feb | Up to 50 cm

White Harveya
Witinkblom
Harveya capensis
(Broomrape family – Orobanchaceae)

An erect, slender, silky-hairy **parasitic** herb.
Leaves: Small, scale-like, reddish green.
Flower head: Delicate white flowers, which can have a pinkish tinge to the outside of the petals. Buds are pink. Stalkless or short-stalked flowers, each having 5 wavy petals and a yellow-tinged keyhole-shaped throat, grow in a loose terminal arrangement at the top of a stout stem. The flowers are scented at night.
Distribution: Occasional.
Habitat: Rocky sandstone mountain slopes.
Notes: The flowers turn black when dried or pressed and were used by early settlers as an ink, hence inkblom.

Aug–Sep | Up to 40 cm

Rose-flowered Sundew
Snotrosie
Drosera cistiflora
(Sundew family – Droseraceae)

A soft, weakly erect, sticky **perennial** with unbranched, leafy stems.
Leaves: Slender, stalkless leaves of varying shapes are scattered up the stem. They appear to be hairy and sticky, covered in red or pale hairs with knob-like glands. The **basal** leaves are not always present.
Flower head: Large, solitary or few in a terminal **inflorescence**: colours mainly pale rose but can be white, with a dark green to black centre and bright orange **anthers**.
Distribution: Common in suitable locations.
Habitat: On well-drained slopes or temporary seepages.

Ash Flower
Wilde Sewejaartjie
Petalacte coronata
(Daisy family – Asteraceae)

An attractive, small, low-growing, greyish-white, sparsely branched, intensely woolly plant with white flowers.
Leaves: Semi-erect, inversely lance-shaped.
Flower head: Looks like ultra-miniature white roses; the grey-white flowers are borne in a round flower cluster.
Distribution: Frequent in Silvermine; occasional on Table Mountain.
Habitat: On dry sandstone slopes.

| Up to 50 cm | Jun–Oct |

Curly-leaved Strawflower
Helichrysum patulum
(Daisy family – Asteraceae)

A straggling, much-branched, woolly shrub or shrublet.
Leaves: Stalkless, white-woolly, paddle-shaped; spaced out up a stout flower stem.
Flower head: Bell-shaped, pale yellow flowers, ringed by white round-tipped **bracts**, cluster in a mass display at the top of the flower stalk.
Distribution: Common.
Habitat: In localised patches on open parts of the mountain and vlei edges.

| Up to 70 cm | Sep–Feb |

Sticky Heath
Taaiheide
Erica physodes
(Erica family – Ericaceae)

A sturdy, erect, dense shrublet with spreading branches.
Leaves: Long, round-pointed leaves.
Flower head: Translucent white, small, sticky balloon-like flowers hang down on little flower stalks in threes or fours at ends of side or main branches; they can appear pale greyish green because of their darker inner **anthers**.
Distribution: Occasional.
Habitat: Prefers moist western to southwestern rocky upper slopes.
Notes: Widespread on Silvermine plateau, south of Constantiaberg.

| Up to 70 cm | May–Aug |

CM

Mar–Jun | Up to 50 cm

Dogface
Hondegesig
Trichocephalus stipularis
(Phylica family – Ramnaceae)

A stout, much-branched shrublet with a dark coloured stem.
Leaves: Long, narrow, alternate, ascending, lance-shaped; leaf edges rolled down.
Flower head: Solitary, small, honey-scented pink flowers, densely woolly-white on the outside, are borne at the top of thick, branched stems. Flowers are tightly clustered together.
Distribution: Common.
Habitat: Sandy lower slopes.

CM

Aug–May | Up to 50 cm

African Stachys
Katbossie
Stachys aethiopica
(Mint family – Lamiaceae)

A sprawling **perennial** with bristly 4-sided stems.
Leaves: Egg-shaped to triangular, toothed.
Flower head: **Whorls** of 2–6 white or pink to mauve flowers with darker spots.
Distribution: Frequent.
Habitat: Often in shade in **fynbos** and forest edges.
Notes: Also commonly called teebos and woundwort.

CM

Jun–Mar | Up to 60 cm

Sweet Sprayflower
Soetgonna
Struthiola dodecandra
(Daphne family – Thymelaeaceae)

A graceful, erect shrub with wand-like branches.
Leaves: Closely packed, small, long, smooth, hairless, faintly ribbed, lance-shaped leaves **sheathe** the erect stem. Leaves opposite, in 4 rows.
Flower head: White or pink tubular flowers, with 8 petal-like scales at the mouth, grow up the long stem.
Distribution: Locally common.
Habitat: Especially seen on mountain slopes in damp areas.

Gunpowder Plant
Kruitbossie
Silene pilosellifolia
(Carnation family – Caryophyllaceae)

An erect to sprawling **perennial** covered with very fine, short, soft hairs.
Leaves: Variable, **basal** leaves oval; upper leaves narrow, inversely lance-shaped, stalkless, broadening towards the top.
Flower head: White-petalled, deeply notched flowers (rarely purple), widely spaced from each other up a long flower stem. The flowers emerge from a stalkless, long, cyclindrical tube, all facing more or less the same direction.
Distribution: Occasional.
Habitat: In bushes on lower slopes.

| Up to 70 cm | Aug–Jan |

Blombos
Metalasia divergens
(Daisy family – Asteraceae)

A sprawling, white-woolly, densely leaved shrublet.
Leaves: Long, slightly twisted and bending backwards.
Flower head: Small white or pink flowers combine in dense terminal clusters to form a disc-shaped 'head'. The outer **bracts** are brown to reddish.
Distribution: Common.
Habitat: Southern sandstone slopes.

| Up to 70 cm | Aug–Jan |

Strawberry Snakebush
Knoppieslangbos
Stoebe rosea
(Daisy family – Asteraceae)

A stiff, much-branched, densely-leafed shrublet.
Leaves: Tiny needle-like sharp-tipped leaves; crowded, twisting, with rolled up leaf edges, grow closely up the stem.
Flower head: Each flower head is spherical, clusters of pink florets emerging through white feathery pappus bristles at the top of flower **spikes**.
Distribution: Occasional.
Habitat: Sandstone slopes on eastern side of Silvermine and further south. Usually found in high rocky areas catching the Southeaster cloud.
Notes: Endemic to the southern Peninsula.

| Up to 50 cm | Jan–Mar |

Glossary

Anther: The end part of the stamen that contains the pollen (*see illustration opposite*).

Basal: Positioned at, or arising from, the base of the stem.

Bracts: Modified leaves often found around the base of a flower head or rising up and above the flowers to look like petals.

Compound (of leaves): Consisting of two or more separate leaflets – opposite of simple (*see illustration opposite*).

Cormous: Referring to a corm, which is an underground, swollen, bulb-like, food-storing stem, sometimes bearing thin, papery leaves.

Fynbos: A term for fine-leaved, shrub-like vegetation, used to describe the unique vegetation of the Cape Floral Kingdom, such as proteas, ericas, etc.

Geophyte: A plant that has an underground food-storage organ, such as a bulb.

Inflorescence: The flower head, cluster or the arrangement of flowers on a plant.

Insectivorous (of plants): Feeding on insects.

Kloof: An Afrikaans word for ravine or valley.

Lobed (of leaves): Partly divided but not separated.

Parasite (in a botanical context): A plant that obtains all or part of its food from another plant.

Perennial: A plant that lives for several years, flowering annually.

Pinnate (of compound leaves): Having several leaflets arranged in pairs, opposite each other (*see illustration opposite*).

Sheathe: To wrap around and protect, such as a leaf wrapping around a stem.

Simple (of leaves): Having a single, undivided blade – opposite of compound (*see illustration opposite*).

Spike: An upright, unbranched flower stem from which flowers grow, from the bottom up.

Stamen: Male, pollen-producing part of a flower, comprising a stalk (filament) and an anther (*see illustration opposite*).

Stigma: Female reproductive organs of a flower, receptive to pollen grains (*see illustration opposite*).

Strap-shaped/strap-like (of leaves): Elongated and flat, like a belt or strap.

Style: A stalk, arising from the ovary, that bears the stigma in a position where it can receive pollen (*see illustration opposite*).

Succulent: Plant with fleshy, swollen stems and leaves that store water.

Tuber: A swollen stem or root that stores food and water underground.

Whorl: A ring-like arrangement of similar parts coming from a common point (*see illustration opposite*).

FLOWER PARTS

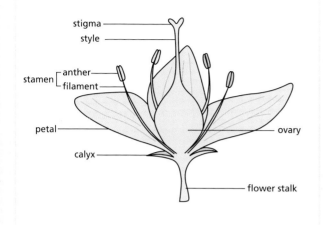

stigma
style
stamen — anther
          filament
petal
calyx
ovary
flower stalk

LEAF TYPES

simple

compound

LEAF ARRANGEMENTS

opposite   alternate   whorl   pinnate   alternately opposite

LEAF SHAPES

sword   lance   oval   spoon   elliptical   round   triangular   wedge

A typical patch of fynbos on the Saddle Path leading to the top of Devil's Peak

Bibliography

We would like to acknowledge the use of the following sources when compiling this book:

Bean, A & Johns, A. 2005. *Stellenbosch to Hermanus. South African Wild Flower Guide 5.* Botanical Society of South Africa, Cape Town

Burman, J. 1991. *The Table Mountain Book.* Human & Rousseau, Cape Town

Cowling, R & Richardson, D. 2000 reprint. *Fynbos.* Fernwood Press, Vlaeberg

Goldblatt, P & Manning, J. 2000. *Cape Plants: A conspectus of the Cape Flora of South Africa.* National Botanical Institute of South Africa & MBG Press, Missouri Botanical Gardens, USA

Goldblatt, P & Manning, J. 2000. *Wild Flowers of the Fairest Cape.* National Botanical Institute of South Africa & ABC Press, Cape Town

Harris, JG & Woolf, M. 2004. *Plant Identification Terminology.* Spring Lake Publishing, USA

Jackson, WPU. 1977. *Wild Flowers of Table Mountain.* Howard Timmins, Cape Town

Jackson, WPU. 1980. *Wild Flowers of the Fairest Cape.* Howard Timmins, Cape Town

Kesting, D. 2003. *Checklist of the Wild Flowers of the Cape Peninsula.* Friends of Silvermine Nature Area

Manning, J. 2003. *Wildflowers of South Africa.* Briza Publications, Pretoria

2007. *Field Guide to Fynbos.* Struik Publishers, Cape Town

2009. Field Guide to *Wild Flowers of South Africa.* Struik Nature, Cape Town

Oliver, I & Oliver, T. 2000. *Ericas of the Cape Peninsula.* National Botanical Institute, Cape Town

Paterson-Jones, C. 1991. *Table Mountain Walks.* Struik Publishers, Cape Town

Rebelo, T. 2000. *Proteas of the Cape Peninsula.* National Botanical Institute, Cape Town

S.A. National Biodiversity Institute websites: **www.plantzafrica.com** and **www.redlist.sanbi.org**

Trinder-Smith, T. 2006. *Wild Flowers of the Table Mountain National Park. South African Wild Flower Guide 12.* Botanical Society of South Africa, Cape Town

Index

Coleonema album 102
Comb Flower 27
Commelina africana 65
Common Babiana 30
Common Bonnet Orchid 82
Common Bulbine 76
Common Butterfly Lily 65
Common Button Daisy 95
Common Buttonbush 101
Common Ground Sugarbush 85
Common Honeybush 72
Common Paintbrush 59
Common Paperflower 105
Common Romulea 39
Common Rosinbush 76
Common Sorrel 74
Common Starheath 100
Common Sugarbush 63
Common Sunshine
  Conebush 105
Common Tickberry 77
Confetti Bush 102
Constantiaberg Heath 49
Corymbium africanum 38
Cotula turbinata 95
Cotyledon orbiculata 62
Crassula capensis 93
  C. coccinea 57
  C. fascicularis 91
  C. pellucida 38
  C. pruinosa 107
Crossyne guttata 51
Cullumia setosa 71
Curly-leaved Strawflower 109
Cyanella hyacinthoides 31
Cyclopia genistoides 72
Cyphia bulbosa 93
  C. volubilis 97
Cyrtanthus ventricosus 61

Dainty Butterfly Bush 40
Dark-eyed Bellflower 34
Dark-eyed Ixia 89
Darktip Heath 49
Diastella divaricata 43
Dilatris corymbosa 37
  D. pillansii 37
Dimorphotheca nudicaulis 102
  D. pluvialis 102
Diosma hirsuta 94
  D. oppositifolia 94
Dipogon lignosus 53
Disa cornuta 30
  D. ferruginea 58
  D. graminifolia 28

D. longicornu 31
D. rosea 57
D. tenuifolia 85
D. uniflora 57
Dischisma ciliatum 94
Disperis capensis 41
Disselblaarluibos 30
Dogface 110
Doublom 45
Drip Disa 31
Drosera cistiflora 108
  D. hilaris 45
  D. trinervia 94
Drumsticks 96

Edmondia sesamoides 105
Empodium plicatum 70
Erepsia anceps 38
Erica abietina subsp. abietina 63
  subsp. atrorosea 58
  subsp. constantiana 49
  E. baccans 45
  E. calycina 101
  E. cerinthoides 60
  E. coccinea 56
  E. corifolia 49
  E. curviflora 55
  E. haematocodon 55
  E. halicacaba 84
  E. hirtiflora 44
  E. imbricata 107
  E. lutea 80
  E. mammosa 59
  E. multumbellifera 49
  E. nevillei 61
  E. nudiflora 43
  E. physodes 109
  E. plukenetii 56
  E. pulchella 46
  E. pyxidiflora 107
  E. urna-viridis 85
Erigeron karvinskianus 92
Eriocephalus africanus 97
Euphorbia caput-medusae 86
Euryops abrotanifolius 76
  E. pectinatus 75
Everlasting Vygie 38

False Slugwort 94
Featherhead 103
Felicia aethiopica 26
  F. fruticosa 37
Ferraria crispa 54
Fire Heath 60
Fire Lily 61

Fish Bean 52
Fivetooth Baboon Cabbage 73
Flat-topped Bitterbush 89
Fleur-de-lys 37
Foetid Cape Tulip 74
Fonteinbos 33
Fountain Bush 33, 35
Fraaibaroe 93
Fragrant Crassula 91
Fringed Aristea 26
Fynblaarmalva 96

Ganna Bush 60
Ganskos 95
Geelbos 105
Geeldisa 85
Geelflappie 70
Geelmargriet 76, 77
Geeloogsuring 64
Geelrysheide 80
Geelsewejaartjie 81
Geelsuring 74
Geissorhiza aspera 27
Geldbeursie 82
Geranium incanum 95
Gladiolus brevifolius 50
  G. carneus 92
  G. debilis 106
  G. maculatus 88
  G. monticola 50, 65
  G. priorii 62
Gnidia juniperifolia 84
  G. oppositifolia 79
  G. pinifolia 98
  G. tomentosa 98
Golden Cowcud 69
Golden Disa 30
Golden Head Cape
  Gorse 72
Gomphocarpus
  cancellatus 87
Gonnabos 60
Grand Duchess Sorrel 52
Grand Stringbark 42
Granny Bonnet 41
Greater Rush Iris 79
Green Satyr Orchid 83
Green Sugarbush 83
Green Violet 90
Grey Pin Buchu 108
Grey Stilbe 104
Grey Tree Pincushion 67
Groenhofiesuikerbos 83
Groentaaiheide 85
Groenviooltjie 90

Hikers climbing up to Maclear's Beacon; Devil's Peak in the background

SM

A scenic view of Hely-Hutchinson and Woodhead dams

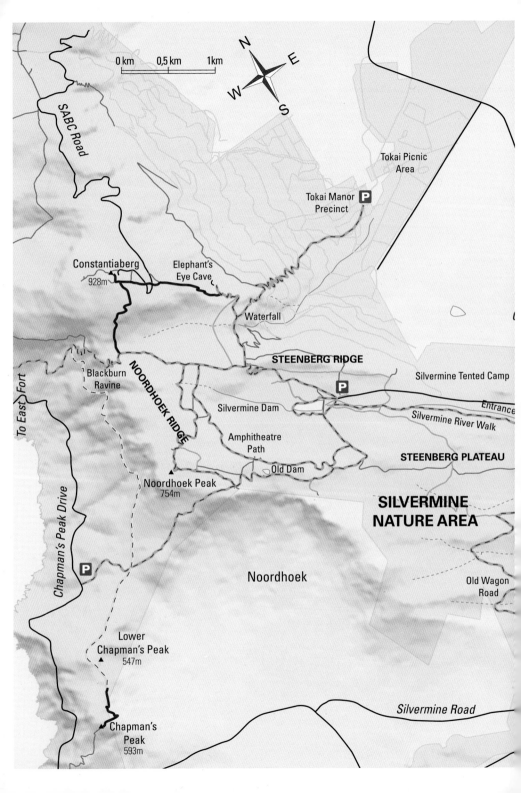